Back to School

Question & Answer Session
with Business Students

Warren Buffett

CONTENTS

Trade Secrets: Mr. Warren Buffett

Discover "trade secrets" and other business gems from the mouth of Mr. Warren Buffett himself in this revealing 2004 Question & Answer session with business students.

Mr. Buffet, one of the most highly acclaimed businesspersons in the United States today, candidly shares some of the inner workings of his Berkshire Hathaway empire, including his long-time partnership with Charlie Munger. A true exposé into a business mind like no other.

WARREN BUFFETT RESPONDS TO QUESTIONS FROM 85 WHARTON STUDENTS ON NOVEMBER 12, 2004

Q: Is it more difficult to find predictable businesses today than it has been historically because the rate of change has increased within most industries? Has the accelerating rate of change within most industries caused you to reassess your buy and hold investment thesis, particularly given the inability for many consumer brands like Coke and Gillette to grow?

A: There are basically two ways to look at change. We see change as the enemy of investments, if it wasn't the richest people would be librarians. Some businesses will change very quickly. We are looking for ones that don't. If you can predict the change then you can become very rich, but the net investment (e.g. from what went on at Kitty Hawk – air flight) to equity investors is a huge negative.

For example, I have a list of over 2000 companies that made automobiles; now the last two, GM and Ford, are in trouble. Hundreds are out of business – many people didn't know that Maytag and Du Pont made automobiles. The net investment for investors has not been a great deal.

We look for certainty of what won't change. You mentioned Gillette. After 100 years, Gillette still has 70% market share, and yet the distribution, product and raw materials are not mysterious. It has survived within our capitalist system and you know its products will be used regularly.

Coke sells 50% of the carbonated beverages worldwide: about 1.3 billion 8-ounce servings, higher than last year and the year before. I guarantee Coke, Wrigleys and Gillette will dominate. The Internet won't change what brands people like.

We are looking for the absence of change. Fruit of the Loom and Haynes together have 80% of boys' underwear in the US. I guess we will keep wearing underwear. Bill Gates welcomes the absence of change; he just doesn't get it in his business. Microsoft and eBay have some moat. If you can identify change, that is great, but it is a lot riskier and so is the chance of our strategy not working. So we look for absence of change.

We don't like to lose money. Capitalism is pretty brutal. We look for mundane products that everyone needs. Patents are the worst way to ensure

demand. There is still plenty of opportunity to find predictable demand. The problem isn't the lack of opportunities; it's the prices.

Q: You wound up the Buffett Partnership in 1969 due in part to the virtual disappearance of investment opportunities for the analyst who stresses quantitative factors. In your view, is today a better investing environment than 1969? How is it better and worse?

A: 1969 was tough. It wasn't pleasant to do. I had grown from $105,000 to $100,000,000. I had a lot of propositions to take over the partnership. If I had a similar partnership I would have closed it around 2000 in the height of the Internet boom.

We were all in REITS in March 2000 when NASDAQ was hitting its high. If I had had a large partnership I would have folded it, but not if it was small. It has to do both with how I feel and how the partners feel. I feel like a jerk (losing on a relative basis) and the jerks are making money. I won't persist in trying to make money when I don't understand what is going on. It is harder to invest and risk other people's money than to invest your own money.

We still get opportunities: for example, we got $8 billion into the Junk Bond thing in 2002 and would have gone up to $22 billion if we had more time. We were buying as fast as we could.

Investing is the world's best game. I was in the department store business – you have to match your competitors – it's a business that throws defensive decisions at you all the time. We want a business with not defensive decisions. Investing is a perfect example. Just watch ball after ball come through and wait for your fat pitch. You can sit and wait for just the right pitch. Harder when you invest in public and the fans are screaming, "swing, you bum."

But at your age, you can fool around with small money and I see things to do there.

Q: You made an argument for 7% returns over the next decade in Fortune:

Given that (a) profit margins are at least 30% above historical averages, (b) the ratio of prices/GDP is at least 25% above historical averages, and (c) interest rates are 25% below historical averages, assuming mean reversion, wouldn't one conclude that while economic earnings growth plus dividends may be 7%, that we are at an unsustainable valuation plateau?

A: We are near the high-end of the valuation band, but not really at an extreme. I have commented on the market 4 or 5 times in *Forbes* interviews previously (1969, 1974, 1981, and 1977 in *Fortune*). Most of you can say if something is overvalued or undervalued, you can spot the occasional extreme cases.

There is a big band of valuation and the idea is to calibrate extremes. When I look at a business, I look for people with passion. I can recognize a 98 or a 6, not a 63. This rule is good enough in life and investment. You refer to my 2001 article, but returns have not exceeded 7%, so I guess that this is not that precise of a band.

I suspect that stocks are too high now. Nothing is cheap and I am not finding a lot of now but there will be a day when you will be shooting fish in a barrel. The important thing is to be prepared to play heavily when the time comes and that means that you cannot play with everybody.

Q: You have said in the past that you would rather buy a great business at a fair price than a fair business at a great price. If the price is fair to both the buyer and the seller and the buyer does not substantially improve the business, then it would be hard to see how the buyer would obtain superior returns from such an investment if the price already discounts the quality of the business.

Since you clearly look for superior returns can you explain how you buy at a price that is both fair to the seller and still leaves you room for abnormal returns?

A: Periodically the stock market does not price rationally. Great businesses have been sold for ridiculously low prices in the past. Unlike negotiated sale of businesses, the market is like an auction and stocks traded on it are not perceived as ownership shares in business. While the price of farmland or apartments in Nebraska does not to vary a great deal around the mean, and have little chance of having wild aberrations, stock prices on the other hand may sometimes vary by as much as 50% to 100%. Accordingly, there are opportunities to buy stocks in businesses at low value.

So we really try to buy wonderful businesses at ridiculous prices. In the case of *Washington Post*, in 1973 the whole of the company was only selling for $80M (5M shares at $16 each).

This is a business that owns a number of newspapers, four TV stations and several magazines (like *Newsweek*). Most analysts would have agreed that the intrinsic value of the assets was around $400 to $500 million. But you could buy little pieces of the business for much less. Seizing this opportunity, Mr. Buffett purchased around 9% of the shares for $10 million in 20-30 tickets from institutional investors who couldn't sell fast enough because they thought the share prices would keep falling.

They wouldn't have argued that the business was not worth $400 million, just that the stock was going down. Subsequently, Mr. Buffett has steadily increased Berkshire's holding in the company (to around 22%) and today the company is worth about $10 billion dollars.

Making purchases through a negotiated market for entire businesses is different. You may get a decent result. These transactions are to a mild degree affected by the auction market. As Peter Lynch often says, companies will cut the flowers and water the weeds – when a company is in trouble it often sells the crown jewels.

Q: What value would you personally attach to $1 received 1 year from today with 100% certainty?

A: It depends on how much purchasing power $1 dollar has in one year. You need to find the present value of that $1 dollar, using the discount rate (i.e., treasuries of equivalent maturity). It is very similar to analyzing the stream of a company's earning flow. How much long term earnings flow you would like to have using the discount rate? Also, you need to be aware of whether the interest rates over the medium-to-long term will change quite big or not.

Your expectation of the "normal" interest rate will drive what discount rate you apply to the streams of a Japanese company in the mid-1990s, for example. If you think the interest rate will rise sharply, and do not want to buy long-term bonds, you need to think about whether you like to buy the company's long-term earnings yield. If you do like long-term bonds, STRIPS are a good investment.

Q: This week Eric Rosenfeld recounted the last days of LTCM and your participation in a potential bailout. He believes that if they could have gotten you back on your cell phone in Alaska the bailout would have been consummated: "to this day I think it would've gotten done if he [Mr. Buffett] was in town…however, nobody was willing to put in $4 billion without consulting [Mr. Buffett]". Could you share your version of the story?

A: Eric called me on Sunday while I was playing bridge. I could tell from the sound of his voice that something grave was transpiring. On Monday he was on vacation with Bill Gates in Alaska, so he was negotiating on a satellite phone, while Bill was looking on. Meanwhile the captain kept moving the boat closer to shore so they could see the bears or something. Gates thought the whole situation was very amusing.

On Tuesday, he was at Yellowstone, and negotiating using an intermediary at Goldman Sachs, and finally gave Goldman his terms on Wed morning. He told Peter (GS Banker) to put in the bid - $3bn from Mr. Buffett, $750mm from AIG, and $250mm from GS. He told Peter to sign his name on the (in)famous letter. Peter asked if he was crazy, but Mr. Buffett told him to just do it. So Peter signs my name, John Corzine's and Hank Greenberg's. He figured if he was on the hook, so he might as well sign Hank Greenberg's name. I don't think anybody's signed Hank's name before. I then went on the bus through Yellowstone (out of range for the satellite phone).

John (Merriwether) got $150mm ($250?). But it left a lot to work out between Wednesday and Monday. "If I'd been in NY, we'd have made the deal…that's [description of Eric Rosenfeld's version] a very accurate rendition of what happened."

They [LTCM] and [NY Fed Governor] McDonnough played the hand the way they should have…but I got to see Old Faithful. I've told Bill Gates lots of times he's cost us a lot of money.

I knew the stuff they were doing…these are the kind of positions I would've put on…I think we would have made multiple billions…I've made a lot of money on weekends.

I don't blame him [Merriwether] – he got an extra $150 million.

Q: You and Charlie Munger believe that the easiest person in the world to fool is yourself. Have you been fooling yourself by remaining committed to certain buy and hold doctrines, especially considering they arc alluring because you have to work less since good investments work for you?

A: People believe what they want to believe. Everyone rationalizes their actions. A partner like Charlie can point it out to me. If we have a strength, it is that we think things through and we have the advantage of having each other. We are not influenced by other people. Charlie would say we are successful because we are rational and do our own work.

Paraphrasing Keynes', "The difficulty lies not in the new ideas but in escaping from the old ones," [Mr. Buffett remarked:] The problem is not holding onto the new [ideas]. The problem is escaping from the old. Darwin claimed he had to write down new ideas constantly. His mind would race to find new ideas. But if he did not write down his new findings within 30 minutes his subconscious would wipe them out and revert to old beliefs.

Q: What do you believe is the top thing that will affect our great country's competitiveness in the future and what would you advise be done to address it? (can follow up with health care and social security/pension gap)

A: One of the biggest problems facing the country is weapons of mass destruction. But there isn't much that can be done about the problem (there will always be terrorists).

The trade deficit, of which current account deficit accounts for 90%, is the biggest economic problem facing the U.S. It is very complicated and not covered sufficiently in the debate. Social security and Healthcare are two issues tied in with the issue of the trade deficit.

When there is no trade deficit, there is no net holding by foreigners. Currently government redistributes 22% of the US output to social security and healthcare. And these issues are eternal intra-family political squabbles over the redistribution between those who are producing and those who are not producing? Trade Deficit is a transfer of ownership or IOU on converted ownership, representing $1.8BN of outflow to foreign countries. It can't be easily addressed. If the trade deficit continues at the current rate for the next 6-10 years, foreigners will have a permanent call on 3% of the output.

Can we afford this? Potentially yes. Foreign aid administered after the Marshall Plan post-WWII can be appropriate. However this is an accumulated burden to be paid by future generations because their "parents" didn't want to pay for it. This could play a significant factor in future financial market disruption. "When someone fires in the theater on the stage" with significant amount of assets held by foreigners, along with other things happening at the same time, the trade deficit could be the #1 problem in the next financial event.

On healthcare, you have to rationalize healthcare demand when healthcare costs become higher and higher. The demand structure under the current system is not sustainable. We need to reframe some of the expectations of people and reframe what is the appropriate level of healthcare provisions.

For example: Should we keep everyone alive for their last 3-6 months? Should people get the maximum amount of care to keep healthy? Government needs to ration it through government

14

policy and people's willingness to wait.

Q: Is there a significant portion of the value you generate from the portfolio derived through active investment (e.g., influence on management decision, etc.) If so, what do you think of the role and probability of long-term success of an investment manager with little influence over management decisions, i.e., a passive investor? Has passive investing lost some of its appeal for you because you have been personally disappointed with the management of major American corporations? If so, what implications does that have for America?

A: In short, Charlie and I do not and should not have a significant impact on the management of our companies. You would be surprised how little impact we have on management. They [CEOs] all have different batting stances and know what style works for them. There would be no point for us to tell them to alter their stance as you can still be a good hitter even if you stand different to the next man - we hire them as they are good hitters.

In terms of our influence on the CEO's of our public holdings - we are "toothless tigers". We do not control the company and do never threaten to sell our stakes if our advice is not taken; therefore we are very much toothless tigers.

We are holders of the stock for the long term and therefore do not gain from short-term increases in the price. Moreover, we actually prefer for the price to go down in the near term so we can buy more stock and increase our stake in the company. However, the disclosure rules make it increasingly difficult for us to build up stakes in companies. For instance, we rarely invest in the UK, as there is a 3% disclosure rule so we cannot build a meaningful stake before it becomes public. So historically, we performed much better when the disclosure requirements were less stringent and they have been increased steadily over time.

Our investment in PetroChina was another example of disclosure rules costing us hundreds of millions of dollars. We had to announce our ownership at a 1% level, after which the price shot up.

Stockholders should be able to think and behave like owners. The three things that a shareholder in a public company should focus on are: do you have the right CEO? Does she/he overreach? Are they too focused on acquisitions or empire building and stop thinking on a per share basis? Institutional owners need to focus on these three aspects.

Both Charlie and I say we would make a lot more money if we were anonymous. You'd be surprised how little impact we have on management. They're all different individuals with their own egos, money, and even control. You'd be surprised how much we don't steer them. We have very little influence on their investments, but it doesn't matter because we don't buy and sell. We don't gain anything from the stock price going up. Piggybacking doesn't do much.

It's a big minus to operate in a public arena where people are not likely to follow. I still have 99% of my net worth in Berkshire, but I try to buy some on my own anonymously -- I do much better that way.

We ask for confidential treatment in some areas, but the SEC doesn't allow that often.

Passive investor role: big institutional owners should act and behave like owners. The big thing to worry about is whether the company has the right CEO and if it does, does the CEO overreach even if he's a good manager? The only people who can stop that are the directors and owners...and the directors will only stop it if the owners make a case. CEOs will sometimes do things uneconomic to satisfy primal urges. My instinct is that the institutional investors behave better than they did 10 years ago.

Q: I am also from Omaha. When I tell people at school about your frugal financial approach, they are stunned. What is your specific philosophy about wealth? And how do you think this discipline has contributed to your success running Berkshire?

A: Mr. Buffett feels he was lucky to be born in the US (he won the ovarian lottery). He believes that he's wired in a way that works well in a capitalistic society: he has the innate ability to allocate money. He believes that society has enabled him to earn this money and so he believes that the money should go back to society eventually. He believes in a graduated income tax. Society has contributed to his wealth so they should benefit.

He discussed the effect wealth has on an individual and the effect it has had on his life: It means that he can do whatever he wants to do. He has the luxury to make choices. But, he has no desire to be a greenskeeper- to own a 20-acre property, which requires him to devote time to organizing and maintaining it. Further, spending the next 4 years building a house doesn't appeal to him. He won't find a house where he'd be happier than the one he's live in since '58-59. He has no interest in owning a large yacht- he views this as more of a hassle than anything else. He prefers to use his wealth to do what he wants to do with the people he wants to do it with.

He likes his life. He likes the people he works with - nobody has left Berkshire voluntarily in 15 yrs. He won't buy a business owned by someone he doesn't like.

If one were to ask Charlie why they were successful, he would respond that it was due to "rational decision making" and being able to not depend and focus on what someone else thinks is important. Also stressed that he was very lucky to be born in the country that he was. Likened it to a lottery with a 1 in 50 chance. This is because he is "wired in a way to be very effective" in a large economy where capital allocation skills are needed and highly rewarded. He illustrated the counter example with a quote from Gates saying that if he were born a few thousand years earlier he "would be an animal's lunch".

As for the trappings of wealth, he believes he already lives the life he wants to live. He cautioned against backing into certain behaviors simply because that was what other rich people do. For example, he does not want to own a large boat, as he simply does not derive enough utility out of it to justify the bother that would entail from owning and maintaining one. As it stands, he does benefit from his wealth in that he has the "ultimate luxury", that is to do what he wants to do everyday and he's having more fun than most 74-year-olds. He doesn't want to build a bigger house and he gets to work with people he likes.

Apparently, they like him too as none of the 18 people who work with him at Berk HQ has left in 15 years. He also will not do a deal simply for the money as it would be as perverse as someone already very wealthy marrying for the money. What money has ultimately given him is the power to choose because the luxury to choose is what being wealthy is all about.

Mr. Buffett continued and discussed the middleweight boxing match he watched on PPV at $54.95. He didn't think twice about the cost of it. He talked about how in the not too distant past the fight would have been limited to people at Madison Square Garden whereas the boxers there stood to gain the benefit from an audience of millions because of what society as a whole has enabled.

Therefore he is, and he believes so should the boxers, be in favor of progressive taxes. That is, they are able to make extraordinary incomes because of society and should be willing to contribute a greater share to maintaining it.

Q: It is clear that you would never resort to earnings smoothing for Berkshire. But you do sell insurance products that have helped other companies smooth their earnings, or at least make their problems look less severe. Is there a contradiction in this?

A: The whole idea of insurance is that you pay a premium each year to protect for a disaster every 20 years. The nature of the product is smoothing earnings. You personally do this with your auto insurance. You pay $400 (or $350 if you call Geico!) to protect yourself. Sometimes companies have used it incorrectly, but this is not inherent in the insurance product. If you get into "no risk transfer" deals with insurance you can get called on it. Berkshire Hathaway has written the two biggest retroactive insurance deals.

One when White Mountain bought One Beacon and the other when ACE bought Cigna. Each paid $1.5 billion to reduce charges for old bad cases. Berkshire Hathaway was much better equipped to handle the risk than ACE or White Mountain (who were both stretching to pay for the deals). All of our policies are finite.

There have been some cases of policies with zero risk transfer in the U.S., but they were very limited in the last five years because auditors must now sign off that there is adequate risk transfer and it is not just for accounting purposes. Generally, there is an understanding and a long relationship between the primary insurer and the re-insurer. If the re-insurer gets killed, the primary does not take the business elsewhere. They just build that experience into next year's quote. This is less prevalent now because it is less client-orientated and more transaction oriented because of the introduction of brokers. There is no more relationship development, just a focus on the lowest price.

Q: At our investment management conference a few weeks ago, one panel featured the CIOs from Barclays Global Investors, State Street and Vanguard, and we collectively discussed the use of derivatives in modern portfolio management. We understand you dealt with unknown exposures in a past acquisition, but wonder if you think in this environment certain institutions have the risk control and discipline to use derivatives to effectively mitigate their risks.

Berkshire uses derivatives. There is nothing evil about them per se. It is very hard to control risks without derivatives. But all mismarks on contracts are in the trader's favor, never our favor. These days, there is no money in plain vanilla stuff - the margins are too squeezed - so you get people writing very sophisticated derivatives.

Berkshire is still unwinding many of its positions. General Re had 23,000 contracts 3 yrs ago and 3000 are left. Derivatives are very tough for management. In situations like 9/11, with losses of unknown magnitude, anyone with big equity and big derivatives portfolio (when you don't know what's behind the derivatives) is in trouble. A big downgrade on the company would have followed with margin postings, etc.

Another issue with derivatives is that the incentives of the guy writing the derivates are not aligned with the company. For example, one of the highest paid guys at Gen Re was the guy that wrote complicated contracts - and those contracts were not necessarily good for the company.

Finally, the problem with large derivatives portfolios is that they tend to be directly related to equity positions that company has. This interdependence means that billions of dollars on your balance sheet are dependent on others performance (other equity performance) - not on your own company performance.

"Derivatives are like AIDS - it's not who you slept with, but who they slept with".

Q: You often talk about the importance of investing only with people you like, trust and admire. However, you've bought companies only days after you became aware of them. How do you evaluate the owners and managers of a company before investing?

After mentioning that he's actually bought companies after only brief telephone conversations, Mr. Buffett admitted that "every now and then you miss", but added that, "it's better than the odds of marriage". He went on to say that "sometimes you size up people better with more time", but he didn't sound like he needed much time to recognize the type of character he looks for.

The key question for him when evaluating the management of a potential acquisition target is "do they love the money or the business". His concern is that he monetizes the owner/manager's wealth and that may cause the latter, if he doesn't truly love the business, not to work as hard after he's sold out to Berkshire. He said he looks for the "obvious cases" of owners who truly love their businesses and added that he's mostly been successful (has had "a good batting average") in identifying them.

For those owners, their businesses are their life's work, which Mr. Buffett compared to a painting: "You spent all your life painting this painting. You can sell it to us and see it hanging in a place of honor in a museum. Or you can sell it to an LBO operator and see it hanging in a porn shop.

"I once bought a jewelry business over the phone. I could tell that the current owner was the 'right' type of person. The owner's great grandfather had started the company and I could tell that the owner really loved the business."

Mr. Buffett said that he can usually "size someone up in less than a day". The most important question he poses in buying a business and looking at management is, "Do they love the business?" He phrased it in this way: "If you spend your whole life painting a picture, would you rather have that painting on exhibit at the Metropolitan Museum of Art, or would you rather earn 5% more on the sale of the painting and have it hanging in a porn shop?"

He has had a great batting average in picking companies and people. But he says that "we can't tell with everyone and once in a while we make a mistake."

Q: The profits of financial companies as a % of total US corporate profits is at an all-time high (40%) -- is this just the result of the carry trade, which will end, or perhaps bogus use of derivatives, or is there something more structural changing?

A: The dollar is not overvalued on a purchasing power basis. Macroeconomics is not our usual game, however if some economic facts are screaming at us, we jump on them. We don't usually do junk bonds, however if you cast your eye about, you can always find deals. I don't feel like doing macro bets as much with other people's money as my own. We work with big currencies-- eight of them.

I don't have a view about which will move most against the dollar. My view is that the dollar will weaken. Countries support their own currency-- Japan wanted to keep their currency down which kept the US currency up. I don't know if China or HK will decouple their currency from the US. I like to have earnings in other currencies because they convert into more dollars, however I keep most of our cash in dollars.

WARREN BUFFETT RESPONDS TO QUESTIONS FROM 85 WHARTON STUDENTS ON NOVEMBER 12, 2004

Q: On probabilistic thinking: while we would all love to do it, how does one distinguish between true subjective probabilistic thinking and bias induced guesswork?

A: Of course we try to make decisions based on probability and not guesswork. I agree strongly with the thoughts in Robert Rubin's book (*In An Uncertain World*). It's all probabilities. The one time when Charlie and I have trouble doing this is when it comes to firing people.

I hate doing that and I avoid it as much as possible. We had one manager at one of our companies who developed Alzeimer's disease. It took us a long time to see it, and after we saw it, it took us a long time to act on it. Fortunately, the company still did well even while he had Alzeimer's, so we've developed a new rule around here: Only buy businesses that are so good that someone with Alzeimer's can manage them!

We all think we're doing the former – probabilistic thinking. Mr. Buffett said he tries to always use probabilistic thinking. That's what he likes about the insurance business and investments. We try to think through every decision that comes to us. Some decisions are simple probabilities.

However, Mr. Buffett added that we're human and probabilistic thinking is not always possible. Mr. Buffett said that when dealing with other people, such as firing someone, is a time in his case that he may stray from probabilistic thinking. An example was when Mr. Buffett denied that one employee who ran one of his businesses had Alzheimer's for one year beyond when anyone else would have picked up on it. He said how hard it was for him to fire him, especially since he loved the person but he was just no longer good at the job. He, therefore, unintentionally postponed the decision. Mr. Buffett said he looked for countering evidence because he hates to fire a CEO he likes. He said he will tolerate a lot from someone who has been an associate. Mr.

Buffett then joked that now he buys businesses that even a person with Alzheimer's can run!

One thinks they know when they're getting way from probabilistic thinking, but you cannot always detect it. Mr. Buffett recommended Bob Rubin's book in which he recommends ways to think in the economic world. He concluded that business is all probabilistic thinking but some thinking is better not being calculated, for example in relation to people you love and humans in general.

Q: You said a year or two ago that the ratio of US corporate profits as a % of GDP was historically high, at 6%, and would likely fall. Since then, the ratio has gone up (nearing 8%). Has something structurally changed, or are you confident that the ratio will still fall back?

A: Mr. Buffett responded that he doesn't believe the 8% rate will be sustainable, and he views 6% as a more reasonable figure in the long run. Moreover, he has trouble reconciling high corporate profits % (even at 6% level) with the corresponding figure of federal taxes paid by corporations, which is currently also at a very high level – 1.5% of GDP.

After a brief discussion of corporate profits and corporate taxes as a percentage of GDP, Mr. Buffett shared an interesting view on federal taxation. In a way, federal government owns a special class of stock (let's call it Class AA stock) in every corporation. For example, last year, Berkshire Hathaway paid ~ $3.4 bil. to federal government in relation to this "stock." The more the company reinvests in its business, the higher next year's earnings and tax payments are – i.e. the higher the dividends and the value of the AA stock are). Moreover, at any point in time, the federal government can change the % of earnings to be distributed to it (i.e. change the tax rate). If the government would ever decide to "go public" with a security of future Berkshire Hathaway tax payments, that stock would be very attractive. Wall Street would love it. In fact, at 35% tax rate, that stock could be worth as much as the entire Berkshire Hathaway.

Warren Buffett Lecture "Triology"

(Notre Dame, 1991)

Read excerpts and full transcripts of business lectures from the legendary Mr. Warren Buffett, including the most interesting things Buffett had to say, as well as things you have never heard him say anywhere else! Addressing topics ranging from "Keys to Investment Success," to "Keys to Avoiding Trouble and Leading a Happy Life," this trilogy is a must-read for business-minded people, young and old.

Three Lectures by Warren Buffett to Notre Dame Faculty, MBA Students and Undergraduate Students, Spring, 1991

Highlights

[For those of you who don't have the time to read the entire transcript, we've pulled out some of the highlights – the most interesting things Buffett said and/or the things that we've never heard him say anywhere else.]

Keys to Investment Success

I found some strange things when I was 20 years old. I went through Moody's Bank and Finance Manual, about 1,000 pages. I went through it twice. The first time I went through, I saw a company called Western Insurance Security Company in Fort Scott, Kansas. They owned 92%, at that time, of the Western Casualty and Surety Company. Perfectly sound company. I knew people that represented them in Omaha. Earnings per share $20, stock price $16. (garbled) ... much more than that. I ran ads in the Fort Scott, Kansas paper to try and buy that stock – it had only 300 or 400 shareholders. It was selling at one times earnings, it had a first class [management team]...

... Incidentally, I would say that almost everybody I know in Wall Street has had as many good ideas as I have; they just had a lot of [bad] ideas, too. And I'm serious about that. I mean when I bought Western Insurance Security selling at $16 and earning $20 per share, I put half my net worth into it. I checked it out first – I went down to the insurance commission and got out the convention statements, I read *Best's*, and I did a lot of things first. But, I mean, my dad wasn't in it, I'd only had one insurance class at Columbia – but it was not beyond my capabilities to do that, and it isn't beyond your capabilities.

Now if I had some rare insight about software, or something like that – I would say that, maybe, other people couldn't do that – or biotechnology, or something. And I'm not saying that every insight that I have is an insight that somebody else could have, but there were all kinds of people that could have understood American Express Company as well as I understood it in '62.

They may have been...they may have had a different temperament than I did, so that they were paralyzed by fear, or that they wanted the crowd to be with them, or something like that, but I didn't know anything about credit cards that they didn't know, or about travelers checks. Those are not hard products to understand. But what I did have was an intense interest and I was willing, when I saw something I wanted to do, to do it, and if I couldn't see something to do, to not do anything. By far, the most important quality is not how much IQ you've got. IQ is not the scarce factor. You need a reasonable amount of intelligence, but the *temperament* is 90% of it.

That's why Graham is so important. Graham's book [*The Intelligent Investor*] talks about the qualities of temperament you have to bring to the game, and that is the game.

Require a Statement Before Being Allowed to Buy a Stock

You shouldn't buy a stock, in my view, for any other reason than the fact that you think it's selling for less than it's worth, considering all the factors about the business.

I used to tell the stock exchange people that before a person bought 100 shares of General Motors they should have to write out on a [piece of paper:] "I'm buying 100 shares of General

Motors at X," and multiply that by the number of shares, "and therefore General Motors is worth more than $32 billion," or whatever it multiplies out to, "because ... [fill in the reasons]".

And if they couldn't answer that question, their order wouldn't be accepted.

That test *should be applied*. I should never buy anything unless I can fill out that piece of paper. I may be wrong, but I would know the answer to that.

"I'm buying Coca Cola right now, 660 million shares of stock, a little under $50. The whole company costs me about $32 billion dollars." Before you buy 100 shares of stock at $48 you ought to be able to answer "I'm paying $32 billion today for the Coca Cola Company because..." [Banging the podium for emphasis.] If you can't answer that question, you shouldn't buy it. If you *can* answer that question, and you do it a few times, you'll make a lot of money.

Tests of a Good Business

A couple of fast tests about how good a business is. First question is, "How long does the management have to think before they decide to raise prices?" You're looking at marvelous business when you look in the mirror and say, "Mirror, mirror on the wall, how much should I charge for Coke this fall?" [And the mirror replies, "More."] That's a great business. When you say, like we used to in the textile business, when you get down on your knees, call in all the priests, rabbis, and everyone else, [and say] "Just another half cent a yard."

Then you get up and they say, "We won't pay it." It's just night and day. I mean, if you walk into a drugstore, and you say, "I'd like a Hershey bar." and the man says, "I don't have any Hershey bars, but I've got this unmarked chocolate bar, and it's a nickel cheaper than a Hershey bar," you just go across the street and buy a Hershey bar. *That* is a good business.

The ability to raise prices – the ability to differentiate yourself in a real way, and a real way means you can charge a different price – *that* makes a great business.

I'll try this on the students later: What's the highest price of a daily newspaper in the United States? [Pause] [This is what he said to the students later: Most of you are familiar with it. The highest priced daily newspaper in the United States, with any circulation at all, is the *Daily Racing Form*. It sells about 150,000 copies a day, and it has for about 50 years, and it's either $2.00 or $2.25 (they keep raising prices) and it's essential.

If you're heading to the racetrack and you've got a choice between betting on your wife's birthday, and Joe's Little Green Sheet, and the *Daily Racing Form*, if you're a serious racing handicapper, you want *The Form*. You can charge $2.00 for *The Form*, you can charge $1.50, you can charge $2.50 and people are going to buy it. It's like selling needles to addicts, basically. It's an essential business. It will be an essential business five or 10 years from now.

You have to decide whether horse racing will be around five or 10 years from now, and you have to decide whether there's any way people will get their information about past performances of different horses from different sources. But you've only got about two questions to answer, and if you answer them, you know the business will make a lot of money. *The Form* has huge profit margins, incidentally, wider than any other newspaper. They charge what they want to basically. It's an easy to understand business – so easy to understand.]

There are products like that, and there are products like sheet steel. And they're night and day.

Agony vs. Ecstasy Businesses: Example 1

It does make a difference what kind of a business you get associated with. For that reason I've set forth in this little handout Company A and Company E. I'm not going to tell you for the moment what these companies are. I'm going to tell you one thing about the two companies. One of the companies, to the point of where this cuts off, lost its investors more money than virtually any business in the world.

The other company made its owner more money than virtually any company in the world. So one of these two companies, Company A and Company E, has made one of its owners one of the five wealthiest people in the world, while the other company made its owners appreciably poorer, probably more so than any other company to that point in time.

Now I'll tell you a little bit about these companies (we're leading up to the question of whether the business makes a difference). Company A had thousands of MBAs working for it. Company E had none. I wanted to get your attention. Company A had all kinds of employee benefit programs, stock options, pensions, the works. Company E never had stock options. Company A had thousands of patents – they probably held more patents than just about any company in the United States. Company E never invented anything. Company A's product improved dramatically in this period, Company E's product just sat.

So far, based on what I've told you, does anybody have any idea of which company was the great success, and why?

If you get to buy one of these two companies, and this is all you know, and you get to ask me one question to decide on which one to buy. If you ask me the right question, you will probably make the right decision about the company's stock, and one will make you enormously wealthy.

Both companies make products used every day. They started as necessities, highly useful, nothing esoteric about either one, although company A does have all these patents. There's more technology involved in company A.

[Question from audience: How many companies compete with either one?]

Good question, very good question. In effect, neither company had any competition. And that might differentiate in some cases.

Well, I'll tell you a little more about it. Company A is known as company A because it was in agony, and Company E, as Company E, because it was in ecstasy. Company A is American Telephone and Telegraph. I've omitted eight zeros on the left-hand side, and the American Telephone and Telegraph Company, at the end of 1979, was selling for $10 billion less than the shareholders had either put in or left in the business. In other words, if shareholder's equity was "X" the market value was X minus $10 billion. So the money that shareholders had put in, or left in the business, had shrunk by $10 billion in terms of market value.

Company E, the excellent company, I left off only six zeros. And that happens to be a company called Thompson Newspapers. Thomson Newspapers, which most of you have probably never heard of, actually owns about 5% of the newspapers in the United States. But they're all small ones. And, as I said, it has no MBAs, no stock options – still doesn't – and it made its owner, Lord Thompson. He wasn't Lord Thompson when he started – he started with 1,500 bucks in North Bay, Ontario buying a little radio station but, when he got to be one of the five richest men, he became Lord Thompson.

The telephone company, with the patents, the MBAs, the stock options, and everything else, had one problem, and that problem is illustrated by those figures on that lower left hand column. And those figures show the plant investment in the telephone business. That's $47 billion, starting off with, growing to $99 billion over an eight or nine year period. More and more and more money had to be tossed in in order to make these increased earnings, going from $2.2 billion to $5.6 billion.

So, they got more money, but you can get more money from a savings account if you keep adding money to it every year. The progress in earnings that the telephone company made was only achievable because they kept on shoving more money into the savings account and the truth was, under the conditions of the '70s, they were not getting paid commensurate with the amount of money that they had to shove into the pot, whereas Lord Thompson, once he bought the paper in Council Bluffs, never put another dime in. They just mailed money every year. And as they got more money, he bought more newspapers. And, in fact, he said it was going to say on his tombstone that he bought newspapers in order to make more money in order to buy more newspapers [and so on].

The idea was that, essentially, he raised prices and raised earnings there every year without having to put more capital into the business.

One is a marvelous, absolutely sensational business; the other one is a terrible business. If you have a choice between going to work for a wonderful business that is not capital intensive, and one that is capital intensive, I suggest that you look at the one that is not capital intensive. I took 25 years to figure that out, incidentally.

Agony vs. Ecstasy Businesses: Example 2 (two Berkshire Hathaway companies)

On the next page, I've got a couple of other businesses here. Company E is the ecstasy on the left. You can see earnings went up nicely: they went from $4 million to $27 million. They only employed assets of $17 million, so that is really a wonderful business. On $17 million they earned $27 million, 150% on invested capital. That is a good business. The one on the right, Company A, the agony, had $11 or $12 million tied up, and some years made a few bucks, and in some years lost a few bucks.

Now, here again we might ask ourselves, "What differentiates these companies?" Does anybody have any idea why company E might have done so much better than Company A? Usually somebody says at this point "maybe company E was better managed than company A." There's only one problem with that conclusion and that is, Company E and Company A had the same manager – me!

The company E is our candy business, See's Candies out in California. I don't know how many of you come from the West, but it dominates the boxed chocolate business out there and the earnings went from $4 million to $27 million, and in the year that just ended they were about $38 million. In other words, they mail us all the money they make every year and they keep growing, and making more money, and everybody's very happy.

Company A was our textile business. That's a business that took me 22 years to figure out it wasn't very good. Well, in the textile business, we made over half of the men's suit linings in the United States. If you wore a men's suit, chances were that it had a Hathaway lining. And we made them during World War II, when customers couldn't get their linings from other people. Sears Roebuck voted us "Supplier of the Year." They were wild about us. The thing was, they wouldn't give us another half a cent a yard because nobody had ever gone into a men's clothing store and asked for a pinstriped suit with a Hathaway lining. You just don't see that.

As a practical matter, if some guy's going to offer them a lining for 79 cents, [it makes no difference] who's going to take them fishing, and supplied them during World War II, and was personal friends with the Chairman of Sears. Because we charged 79½ cents a yard, it was "no dice."

See's Candies, on the other hand, made something that people had an emotional attraction to, and a physical attraction you might say. We're almost to Valentine's Day, so can you imagine going to your wife or sweetheart, handing her a box of candy and saying, "Honey, I took the low bid."

Essentially, every year for 19 years I've raised the price of candy on December 26. And 19 years goes by and everyone keeps buying candy. Every ten years I tried to raise the price of linings a fraction of a cent, and they'd throw the linings back at me. Our linings were just as good as our candies. It was much harder to run the linings factory than it was to run the candy company. The problem is, just because a business is lousy doesn't mean it isn't difficult.

In the end, I like to think anyway that if Alfred P. Sloan [the legendary CEO of General Motors during its heyday] came back and tried to run the lining business, it wouldn't make as much money as a good business. The product was undifferentiated. The candy product is differentiated. (Garbled story of Hershey Bar and Coke versus unbranded but modestly cheaper products).

You really want something where, if they don't have it in stock, you want to go across the street to get it. Nobody cares what kind of steel goes into a car.

Have you ever gone into a car dealership to buy a Cadillac and said, "I'd like a Cadillac with steel that came from the South Works of US Steel." It just doesn't work that way, so that when General Motors buys they call in all the steel companies and say, "Here's the best price we've got so far, and you've got to decide if you want to beat their price, or have your plant sit idle."

The Importance of Management: Cap Cities vs. CBS

I put one business in here, CBS versus Cap Cities in 1957, when my friend Tom Murphy took over Cap Cities. They had a little bankrupt UHF station in Albany. They ran it out of a home for retired nuns. And it was very appropriate because they had to pray every day. At that time CBS was the largest advertising medium in the world: $385 million in revenues whereas Cap Cities had $900,000 in revenues. Cap Cities made $37,000 a year and they paid my friend Murph $12,000 a year. CBS made $48 million pretax. Cap Cities was selling for $5 million in the market and priced on the come, while CBS was selling for $500 million.

Now, if you look at the two companies, Cap Cities has a market value of about $7 billion and CBS has a market value of about $2 billion. They were both in the same business, broadcasting. Neither one had, certainly Cap Cities didn't have, any patents. Cap Cities didn't have anything that CBS didn't have. And somehow CBS took a wonderful business that was worth $500 million, and over about 30 years they managed a little increase – peanuts – while my friend Murphy, with exactly the same business, with one little tiny UHF station in Albany, (bear in mind that CBS had the largest stations in New York City and Chicago) and my friend Murph just killed them. And you say, "How can that happen?" And that's what you ought to study in business school. You ought to study Tom Murphy at Cap Cities. And you also ought to study Bill Paley [who was the CEO] at CBS.

We have a saying around Berkshire that "all we ever want to know is where we're going to die, so we'll never go there." And CBS is what you don't want. It's as important not to do what CBS did, and it is important to do what Cap

Cities did. Cap Cities did a lot of things right, but if CBS had done the same things right, Cap Cities would have never come close.

They had all the IQ at CBS that they had at Cap Cities. They had 50 times as many people, and they were all coming to work early and going home late. They had all kinds of strategic planners. They had management consultants. They had more than I can say. Yet they *lost*. They lost to a guy that started out with a leaky rowboat, at the same time the other guy left in the QE II.

By the time they got into New York, the guy in the rowboat brought in more cargo than the QE II did. There's a real story in that. And you can understand broadcasting, so it's really worth studying what two people in the same field did, and why one succeeded so much and one failed.

I couldn't resist kicking in the last page: the only public offering Cap Cities ever made, back in 1957 which raised, as you can see, $300,000. And this was when they were going to buy the station in Raleigh/Durham.

The only public offering of stock the company's every made (aside: they sold us a block of stock when they bought ABC). And if you look very carefully you'll see that the underwriting commission – they took two firms to get this sold – the total underwriting commission was $6,500 bucks.

The Perils of the "Mindless Imitation of One's Peers"

The last thing I want to show you, before we get onto your questions, is an ad that was run June 16, 1969, for 1,000,000 shares of American Motors. This is a reproduction from the *Wall Street Journal* of that day. Now does anybody notice anything unusual about that ad?

[Guesses from audience.]

Everybody in that ad has disappeared. There are 37 investment bankers that sold that issue, plus American Motors, and they are *all* gone. Maybe that's why they call them tombstone ads. Now the average business of the New York Stock exchange in 1969 was 11 million shares. Average volume now is *fifteen* times as large.

Now here's an industry whose volume has grown 15 to 1 in 20 years. Marvelous growth in the financial world. And here are 37 out of 37, and those are some of the biggest names on Wall Street, and some of them had been around the longest, and 37 out of 37 have disappeared. And that's why I say you ought to think about [the long-term durability of a business?] because these people obviously didn't.

These were run by people with high IQs, by people that worked ungodly hard. They were people that had an intense interest in success. They worked long hours. They *all* thought they were going to be leaders on Wall Street at some point, and they all went around, incidentally, giving advice to other companies about how to run their business. That's sort of interesting.

You go to Wall Street today, and there's some company the guy hadn't heard of two weeks before and he's trying to sell you. He will lay out this computer run of the next 10 years, yet he doesn't have the faintest idea of what his own business is going to earn next week!

Here are a group of 37. And the question is, how can you get a result like that? That is not a result that you get by chance. How can people who are bright, who work hard, who have their own money in the business – these are not a bunch of absentee owners – how can they get such a bad result? And I suggest that's a good thing to think about before you get a job and go out into the world.

I would say that if you had to pick one thing that did it more than anything else, it's the mindless imitation of one's peers that produced this result. Whatever the other guy did, the other 36 were like a bunch of lemmings in terms of following. That's what's gotten all the big banks in trouble for the past 15 years. Every time somebody big does something dumb, other people can hardly wait to copy it. If you do nothing else when you get out of here, do things *only* when they make sense to you. You ought to be able to write,

"I am going to work for General Motors because... " "I am buying 100 shares of Coca Coals stock because..." And if you can't write an intelligent answer to those questions, don't do it.

I proposed this to the stock exchange some years ago: that everybody be able to write out, "I am buying 100 shares of Coca Cola Company, market value $32 billion, because..." and they wouldn't take your order until you filled that thing out.

I find this very useful when I write my annual report. I learn while I think when I write it out. Some of the things I think, I find don't make any sense when I start tying to write them down and explain them to people. You ought to be able to explain why you're taking the job you're taking, why you're making the investment you're making, or whatever it may be. And if it can't stand applying pencil to paper, you'd better think it through some more.

People in that ad did a lot of things that could not have stood that test. Some *major* bankers in the United States did a lot of things that could not meet that test. One of the bankers in the United States, who's in plenty of trouble now, bragged a few years ago he never made a loan. And, from the way things are starting to look, he's never going to collect on one either.

You should not be running one the major banks in the United States without having made loans. I mean, you learn about human nature, if nothing else, when you make loans.

The Perils of Leverage

The question is whether LBOs and junk bonds and so on have hurt the country in some fundamental way in terms of its competitiveness vis-a-vis the world. I wouldn't go that far, but I think on balance it's been a huge minus on the financial scene. Extreme leverage has been, generally speaking, a net minus.

The analogy has been made (and there's just enough truth to it to get you in trouble) that in buying some company with enormous amounts of debt, that it's somewhat like driving a car down the road and placing a dagger on the steering wheel pointed at your heart. If you do that, you will be a better driver; that I can assure you. You will drive with unusual care. You also, someday, will hit a small pothole, or a piece of ice, and you will end up gasping. You will have fewer accidents, but when they come along, they'll be fatal. Essentially, that's what some of corporate America did in the last 10 years. And it was motivated by huge fees. And it was motivated by greed.

The most extreme case I saw was a television station. About three years ago, a television station in Tampa sold for an amount where, when they had to borrow the money, the interest amounted to more than the total sales of the station.

If everybody donated their labor, if they donated their programming, if they donated their utilities, they still wouldn't have enough to pay the interest. They went crazy. And you can buy those bonds at 15 cents on the dollar. Charlie Keating's enterprise [Lincoln Savings and Loan Association in California, which became the nation's largest thrift failure] had a bunch of them too. There's a lot of crazy stuff that went on in the last five or six years.

The fees on that deal, they paid $365 million for the station, they borrowed $385 million and you can guess where the extra money went. It went into the pockets of the people who put the deal together.

Donald Trump and the Perils of Leverage

Where did Donald Trump go wrong? The big problem with Donald Trump was he never went right. He basically overpaid for properties, but he got people to lend him the money. He was terrific at borrowing money. If you look at his assets, and what he paid for them, and what he borrowed to get them, there was never any real equity there. He owes, perhaps, $3.5 billion now, and, if you had to pick a figure as to the value of the assets, it might be more like $2.5 billion. He's a billion in the hole, which is a lot better than being $100 in the hole because if you're $100 in the hole, they come and take the TV set. If you're a billion in the hole, they say, "Hang in there, Donald."

It's interesting why smart people go astray. That's one of the most interesting things in business. I've seen all sorts of people with terrific IQs that end up flopping in Wall Street or business because they beat themselves. They have 500 horsepower engines, and get 50 horsepower out of them. Or, worse than that, they have their foot on the brake and the accelerator at the same time. They really manage to screw themselves up.

...I would suggest that the big successes I've met had a fair amount of Ben Franklin in them. And Donald Trump did not.

Life Tends to Snap You at Your Weakest Link

One of the things you will find, which is interesting and people don't think of it enough, with most businesses and with most individuals, life tends to snap you at your weakest link. So it isn't the strongest link you're looking for among the individuals in the room. It isn't even the average strength of the chain. It's the weakest link that causes the problem.

It may be alcohol, it may be gambling, it may be a lot of things, it may be nothing, which is terrific. But it is a real weakest link problem.

When I look at our managers, I'm not trying to look at the guy who wakes up at night and says " $E = MC^2$ " or something. I am looking for people that function very, very well. And that means not having any weak links. The two biggest weak links in my experience: I've seen more people fail because of liquor and leverage – leverage being borrowed money.

Donald Trump failed because of leverage. He simply got infatuated with how much money he could borrow, and he did not give enough thought to how much money he could pay back.

Keys to Avoiding Trouble and Leading a Happy Life

You really don't need leverage in this world much. If you're smart, you're going to make a lot of money without borrowing. I've never borrowed a significant amount of money in my life.

Never. Never will. I've got no interest in it. The other reason is I never thought I would be way happier when I had 2X instead of X. You ought to have a good time all the time as you go along. If you say, "I'm taking this job – I don't really like this job but in three years it will lead to this," forget it. Find one you like right now.

Full Transcripts
Lecture to Faculty

Thank you. When you asked me what I did, in this year's annual report I tried to describe what I do...

[Told Beemer the Clown story; excerpt from 1990 Berkshire Hathaway annual letter:

Much of the extra value that exists in our businesses has been created by the managers now running them. Charlie and I feel free to brag about this group because we had nothing to do with developing the skills they possess: These superstars just came that way. Our job is merely to identify talented managers and provide an environment in which they can do their stuff. Having done it, they send their cash to headquarters and we face our only other task: the intelligent deployment of these funds.

My own role in operations may best be illustrated by a small tale concerning my granddaughter, Emily, and her fourth birthday party last fall. Attending were other children, adoring relatives, and Beemer the Clown, a local entertainer who includes magic tricks in his act.

Beginning these, Beemer asked Emily to help him by waving a "magic wand" over "the box of wonders." Green handkerchiefs went into the box, Emily waved the wand, and Beemer removed blue ones. Loose handkerchiefs went in and, upon a magisterial wave by Emily, emerged knotted. After four such transformations, each more amazing than its predecessor, Emily was unable to contain herself. Her face aglow, she exulted: "Gee, I'm really good at this."

And that sums up my contribution to the performance of Berkshire's business magicians - the Blumkins, the Friedman family, Mike Goldberg, the Heldmans, Chuck Huggins, Stan Lipsey and Ralph Schey. They deserve your applause.]

We've never had a meeting of our managers. The fellow that runs the candy company we bought 19 years ago [See's Candies], last year came to Omaha because he and his wife wanted to see what the annual meeting was like, but he'd never come to Omaha [before that]. We've never had a meeting with his board. We moved the company's headquarters from Los Angeles to San Francisco because his wife liked living in San Francisco better than Los Angeles. We adapt our operations to the people that run our businesses.

We've got a uniform company in Cincinnati, Fechheimers. Does about $100 million. Bought it about five years ago. A fellow read the annual report where I list what I'm looking for. I run an ad in the annual report (I believe in advertising) and this fellow walked in and said, "I fit those parameters, and the business does" and we made a deal with him. I've never visited Cincinnati. I've not seen that plant. It may be a [hoax] – for all I know, he makes up these little reports every five (garbled). But he sends me cash, and I like that.

So it's a very peculiar operation. I bought a business eight years ago from an 89-year-old woman who started with $500, never put in another dime, and it was making about $12 million before taxes (about $18 million now). She doesn't know what accruals are; she doesn't know any of that sort of thing.

She got mad at her grandsons, who work at the company, a few years ago, so she quit and went into competition with us. This taught me that the next time I buy a business from an 89-year-old woman, I'm getting a non-compete agreement. This woman now runs another successful business.

She's a marvelous woman. She walked out of Russia. She landed in Seattle with a tag around her neck. She couldn't speak a word of English. Fort Dodge, Iowa was where her relatives were. She got to Fort Dodge about 1920 or 1919, and they didn't have a penny.

She brought over seven siblings, as well as her mother and father, and that took her eight or 10 years, sending $50 bucks at a time. She made it selling used clothing. She started this company in 1937 with $500. She was boycotted by most of the suppliers, the main carpet companies in town.

They took her into court on violation of fair trade laws. When she got before the judge, Judge Chase, she said, "Judge, I paid $3 a yard for this. Brandeis (a carpet store) paid $3 too. They sell it for $6.99. I sell it for $3.99. Tell me how much you want me to rob people. If you tell me to rob them $1 a yard, I'll charge them $4.99." The newspaper picks up all this and the judge comes in and buys $1,400 worth of carpet. She beat them in court four times and every time she killed them.

This company is now the largest home furnishings store, by a factor of 2 to 1, over any home furnishings store in the United States. It does $160 million from one location. That one store makes about $18 million pretax. It has a 500,000 square foot warehouse (garbled).

That woman, who got an honorary degree from NYU business school about five or six years ago (garbled), you cannot beat her record. If you tell her this room is 38 by 16, she will tell you how many square yards it is, just like that. And she's 97. She'll tell you how many yards it is at $5.99, the extension, and she'll have the sales tax, and she'll knock off something if you're a nice fresh face. And that's it. She can do it all as fast as I've said that. She sold me the business in 30 seconds. She talked to me and told me how much she'd wanted. She'd never had an audit. I didn't need an audit. Her word was better than the Bank of England.

We make all our deals that way. Our total legal and accounting fees on that deal, which was a $60 million deal, we had to file a 10Q with the SEC, we had to file a Hart-Scott-Rodino filing, our total legal and accounting fee came to $1,400 bucks. All on one page. There's a mark where her name is. It says, "Mrs. B on behalf of herself and her children." She only owned 20% of the business. She made her mark, and the deal was cut.

All our deals are done like that. We've made all our deals, essentially, on the first contact. We never get warranties; we never get anything.

These people are rich, and we have to figure out if they're the kind of people to keep working after they've sold out. We have to decide if they're working because they love the business, or because they love money. And, if they love

money, they're not of any use to us because I can't give them enough money after they've got all the money [from selling us] their business.

They've got to love the business. I would say that if we do anything very well at Berkshire, it's spotting the kind of people that, after they are very rich, will work even harder. We get no budgets from them. We have one board of directors meeting a year, which follows the shareholders meeting. No one has to come in. All they have to do is run the businesses. And we've got a bunch of those now.

They mail me the money – that's the second part of their job. And it's my job to allocate capital. They can do whatever makes sense in the candy business, or the newspaper business, but they don't have to go out and do a bunch of foolish things. We like businesses that generate cash. Sometimes we have something to do with it, sometimes we don't. We prefer to buy businesses with it but if we can't buy businesses with it, we buy pieces of businesses called stocks.

Our biggest holdings: we own 7% of the Coca Cola Company,

worth about $2 billion. Your Chairman here [referring to the President of Coca Cola, Don Keough, who was also Chairman of Notre Dame's board] used to live across the street from me in Omaha 30 years ago when he was a salesman for Butternut Coffee.

He had six kids, making $200 bucks a week, and starving to death. He was telling at lunch how he went into his boss one day, and told him about the six kids, about the parochial school, paying him $200 bucks a week and "it just ain't easy pal", and while he was doing this his boss, Paul Gallagher [the owner of Butternut Coffee], reached into his desk and pulled out a scissors and starting cutting strands off his fraying shirt. He walked away. Fortunately, things have improved some.

We have 7% of Coke. There are 660 million eight-ounce servings of Coca Cola products being served around the world today, so in effect, we've got a 45 million soft drink business with our 7%. We think of businesses that way. I say to myself, "Just increase the price a penny and that's another $450,000 a day for Berkshire." I mean, it's a nice sort of thing. When I go to bed at night I figure that by the time I wake up 200 million Cokes will have been consumed. We've got some Gillette too, and every night I think about two billion plus men's hair growing and four billion women's legs with hair. It goes all night when I sleep.

So we buy businesses I can understand, whether all of them or small parts of them. We never buy anything that I don't think I can understand. I may be wrong about whether I understand it or not, but we've never owned a share of a technology company. There's all kinds of businesses I don't understand. I don't worry about that. Why should I (garbled). You mentioned *Cities Service Preferred*; I didn't understand that very well when I bought it. Ever since I met Ben Graham, I was 19. I read his book when I was 18. It made nothing but sense to me.

Buy pieces of businesses you can understand when they're offered to you for quite a bit less than they're worth. That's all there is to it. That's what we try to do with 100% of the business, 7% of the business, or whatever. My partner Charlie Munger and I have been together for about 15 years, and that's all we do. And we'll never do anything else.

Mrs. B is that way. I couldn't have given her $200 million worth of Berkshire Hathaway stock when I bought the business because she doesn't understand stock. She understands cash. She understands furniture. She understands real estate. She doesn't understand stocks, so she doesn't have anything to do with them. If you deal with Mrs. B in what I would call her circle of competence... She is going to buy 5,000 end tables this afternoon (if the price is right). She is going to buy 20 different carpets in odd lots, and everything else like that [snaps fingers] because she understands carpet. She wouldn't buy 100 shares of General Motors if it was at 50 cents a share.

I would say that the most important thing in business, and investments, which I regard as the same thing, from our standpoint, is being able to accurately define your circle of competence. It isn't a question of having the biggest circle of competence. I've got friends who are competent in a whole lot bigger area than I am, but they stray outside of it.

In that book *Father, Son & Co.* [subtitle: My Life at IBM and Beyond] you may have read, that Tom Watson Junior recently wrote, he quoted his father as saying, "I'm no genius. I'm smart in spots but I stay around those spots." And that's all there is to it in investments – and business. I always tell the students in business school they'd be better off when they got out of business school to have a punch card with 20 punches on it. And every time they made an investment decision they used up one of those punches, because they aren't going to get 20 great ideas in their lifetime.

They're going to get five, or three, or sever, and you can get rich off five, or three, or seven. But what you can't get rich doing is trying to get one every day. The very fact that you have, in effect, an unlimited punch card, because that's the way the system works, you can change your mind every hour or every minute in this business, and it's kind of cheap and easy to do because we have markets with a lot of liquidity – you can't do that if you own farms or [real estate] – and that very availability, that huge liquidity which people prize so much is, for most people, a curse, because it tends to make them want to do more things than they can intelligently do.

If we can do one intelligent thing a year we are ecstatic. You can negotiate us down to one every two or three years without working very hard. That's all you need. You need very few good ideas in your lifetime. You have to be willing to have the discipline to say, "I'm not going to do something I don't understand." Why should I do something I don't understand? That's why I find it an advantage to be in Omaha instead of New York. I worked in New York for a few years, and people were coming up to me on the corner and whispering in my ear all the time. I was getting excited all the time. I was a wonderful customer for the brokers.

Let's talk about what you're interested in.

That's a problem. It helps to have the efficient market out there. It's very nice to have people out there saying, "None of this does any good." It's a real advantage to have. I don't think it's as strong now, but you really had the revealed truths, for a decade or so, saying it didn't do any good to think.

Investments presumably means businesses, too. And once you say investments are all priced efficiently, you presumably have to go on and say businesses are priced efficiently, and you're just throwing darts all the time.

If this group were a bunch of chess players, or a bunch of bridge players, and they were all convinced that it did not pay to think about what to do, you'd have an enormous advantage. We've had tens of thousands of students in business schools taught that it's [a waste of time to think].

48

You mentioned the five-sigma event; actually it was Bill Sharpe out at Stanford many years ago. My friend Charlie says that, "as the record gets longer it's easier to add a sigma than it is to reevaluate the theory." Which is sort of true. I think it was Ken Galbraith that said, "Economists are most economical about ideas. They make the ones they learn in school last a lifetime."

The market generally is pretty efficient. You take the 30 stocks in the Dow and a bunch of very smart minds all looking at them and having the same information and most of the time, not all of the time, they'll be priced efficiently. So what? You only have to be right a few times. Sometimes it's very strange things. Sometimes it's panic (garbled).

In '74 you could have bought the Washington Post when the whole company was valued at $80 million. Now at that time the company was debt free, it owned the *Washington Post* newspaper, it owned *Newsweek*, it owned the CBS stations in Washington D.C. and Jacksonville, Florida, the ABC station in Miami, the CBS station in Hartford/New Haven, a half interest in 800,000 acres of timberland in Canada, plus a 200,000-ton-a-year mill up there, a third of the *International Herald Tribune*, and probably some other things I forgot. If you asked any one of thousands of investment analysts or media specialists about how much those properties were worth, they would have said, if they added them up, they would have come up with $400, $500, $600 million.

Bob Woodward one time said to me, "Tell me how to make some money," back in the '70s, before he'd made some money himself on a movie and a book. I said, "Bob, it's very simple. Assign yourself the right story. The problem is you're letting Bradley assign you all the stories. You go out and interview Jeb Magruder." I said, "Assign yourself a story. The story is: what is the Washington Post Company worth? If Bradley gave you that story to go out and report on, you'd go out and come back in two weeks, and you'd write a story that would make perfectly good sense. You'd find out what a television station sells for, you'd find out what a newspaper sells for, you'd evaluate temperament." I said, "You are perfectly capable of writing that story. It's much easier than finding out what Bill Casey is thinking about on his deathbed. All you've got to do is assign yourself that story."

"Now, if you come back, and the value you assign the company is $400 million, and the company is selling for $400 million in the market, you still have a story but it doesn't do you any good financially. But if you come back and say it's $400 million and it's selling for $80 million, that screams at you. Either you are saying that the people that are running it are so incompetent that they're going to blow the $400 million, or you're saying that they're crooked and that they're operating Bob Vesco style. Or, you've got a screaming buy when you can buy dollar bills for 20 cents. And, of course, that $400 million, within eight or 10 years, with essentially the same assets, [is now worth] $3 or $4 billion."

That is not a complicated story. We bought in 1974, from not more than 10 sellers, what was then 9% of the Washington Post Company, based on that valuation. And they were people like Scudder Stevens, and bank trust departments. And if you asked any of the people selling us the stock what the business was worth, they would have come up with an answer of $400 million. And, incidentally, if it had gone down to $60 or $40 million, the beta would have been higher of course, and it would have therefore been [viewed as] a riskier asset. There is no risk in buying the stock at $80 million. If it sells for $400 [million] steadily, there's much more risk than if it goes from $400 million to $80 million.

But that's all there is to business. But now you say, "I don't know how to evaluate the Washington Post." It isn't that hard to evaluate the Washington Post. You can look and see what newspapers and television stations sell for. If your fix is $400 and it's selling for $390, so what? You can't [invest safely with such a small margin of safety]. If your range is $300 to $500 and it's selling for $80 you don't need to be more accurate than that. It's a business where that happens.

At the time we bought Coca Cola just two years ago, [we ended up buying] 7% of the company. We paid a billion dollars, so we were paying $14 billion, essentially, for the whole thing. You can sit down in five minutes – I mean, everybody here understands Coca Cola.

If Philip Morris were to buy Coca Cola that day, they would have paid $30 billion. And they wouldn't have sold it for that. And you wouldn't have sold it for that. The company is actually repurchasing stock at the time. So, in effect, they're buying for you. They're buying out your partners, at 50 cents on the dollar or less, which is a magnificent sort of business, and there are no morals to it. It's an easy business. There's no doubt about it.

I don't know a thing now that I didn't know at 19 when I read that book. For eight year prior to that I was a chartist. I loved all that stuff. I had charts coming out my ears. Then, all of a sudden a fellow explains to me that you don't need all that. Just buy something for less than it's worth.

The world, generally, is treated much more favorably in relation to buying businesses than we are because we're restricted now to buying big businesses, or pieces of big businesses. And that is a big disadvantage. As Charlie says, "There could be worse things."

You'll find this interesting. At market, we've probably got $7 or $8 billion in equities. In 1970, Berkshire had about $15 million in equities. We owned more securities then than we own now. We do not have it solved by buying more things. Every now and then we find something. In our annual report this year [we disclosed that] we made two large purchases. Each one was $300 or $400 million. Every now and then you'll get an opportunity. And when they come, they come for 15 minutes [I think that's what he said]. Some days it's raining gold. Not very often, but when it is, you've got to be out there. And that will happen periodically. It'll happen, but you can't make it happen. In the meantime, you let the cash pile up if that's what happens.

[Question from audience: How many of your investment ideas are pitched to you by others?]

Practically none. The *Wall Street Journal* is my deal source. There are 1,700 or 1,800 of America's companies that I'm generally familiar with – a good many of them, and every day they move around the prices of them. So here's a business broker's office, if you want to call it that. And sometimes they change them pretty dramatically, like October 19th of '87. But they change them dramatically. And that is a great start. Any business that I buy will be measured against the yardstick of that business brokers office in Section C of the *Wall Street Journal*.

In terms of deals, our standards are such that very few are going to meet it. We are much more likely to find one from an owner, who owns the business himself, who wants to sell it to someone like us, and if they want to sell to someone like us, we're the only one like us. I can promise them, a) since I control Berkshire, the only one who can double cross them or lie to them is me. If they start with the XYZ company, XYZ can be taken over tomorrow, the directors can get a new strategic [plan] tomorrow, they can have McKinsey come in and tell them to do something different tomorrow. And no one can really make them a promise there like I can make them a promise. I can tell them exactly what will and won't happen when I make a deal, and to some people that is very important.

It's important to me with Berkshire. I've got a lot of things in my will about (garbled) is better, and all kinds of things. I care where that goes, the same way I care about anything else I've spent my lifetime working on. When I run into somebody like that, we've got an advantage. To some extent, they know about us, and I'll hear about them, but not very many. They're very few. And they're usually older when it happens. Sometimes they've got other members of the family in the business that are inactive and want to take the money out. We've arraigned, in three of our businesses, with younger generations to take 18%, or 15%, or 20% of the equity. We can do a lot of things, in terms of meeting objectives, that some owners may [appreciate] although most owners [don't have complex requirements]. But it is not a question of answering the phone and taking an investment banker's call.

In terms of marketable securities or new offerings, we've never bought anything [that's been pitched to us by an investment banker or broker]. We don't pay any attention to investment bankers or brokers. It's not an efficient use of our time [to read their] reports. We read hundreds and hundreds of annual reports every year. I own 100 shares of everything. I find this much more reliable than asking to be put on a mailing list.

I was reading the Gillette report. I noticed that they'd bought in a bunch of stock. I'd known that before. Their net worth was below zero, which doesn't make a lot of difference, but I thought it might bother them, with the kind of history the company had. So I saw the name of a director that was a friend of mine, Joe Sisco. I called Joe and said, "I don't know the people up there, but if they're interested in doing something in the way of financing I would be interested and, if they're not, I'll never bother them." Joe called me back in a couple of days, Coleman Mockler and I got together and we put $600 million in.

We bought Scott Fetzer (World Book, Kirby Vacuum, and all sorts of things). It had been mixed up for about a year and a half, being sort of in play. I'd never met Ralph Schey, never talked to him on the phone, never had any contact with him at all. And I wrote him a letter that said, "Here's our annual report. If you're interested in talking to me we'll pay cash, our check will clear, it will be a one-page deal. If you're not interested, I'll never bother you again, and you'll never hear again, and throw the letter out." He called me back. We met in Chicago on a Sunday and we made a deal that night, [signed the documents the] next week, and that was it.

[Question from audience: What was it about Gillette that appealed to you?]

I can understand (garbled) and shaving, the price flexibility, what I call the moat around the business. The most important thing with me in evaluating businesses is figuring out how big the moat is around the business. I want to know how big the capital is on the inside and then I want to know how big the moat is around it. What you love is big capital and a big moat. Obviously. World Book has a real moat. Kirby has a real moat. You can figure that out if you [studied] the distribution process and everything.

I've been in the textile business. We made half of the men's linings in the United States for 25 years.

Gillette was the kind of business we'd put capital into on the right basis.

One of the biggest early things was American Express back in 1962 at the time of the salad oil scam. There was a guy named De Angelis in Bayonne, New Jersey.

American Express had a field warehousing company which was a tiny, tiny, little subsidiary, with $12 [million] in capital. The field warehousing company's job was to certify that inventories really existed. That was their job. They stuck their name on it, and you could take those certificates that said there was a given amount of whatever there was, and you could borrow against these certificates. Tino De Angelis had this tank farm about 15 miles from lower Manhattan. And the American Express field warehousing company authenticated the existence of salad oil in these tanks. And, at one time, they were authenticating the existence of more salad oil than the Department of Agriculture, in its monthly reports, was saying existed in the United States.

But they never told us of that discrepancy. Late in 1962, right at the time Kennedy was assassinated, within a day or two, the thing blew. A couple of New York Stock Exchange firms went broke – Ira Haupt, (garbled), maybe one other – because they lent on these phony certificates.

And American Express, which never even thought of this little field warehousing operation - it was nothing, compared to their money order business, credit card, and travel - all of a sudden, they've got this little subsidiary, not the parent company, but the subsidiary, that was on the hook for tens and tens of millions of dollars, and nobody knows how much. And that is the nice thing about fraud (garbled)…

There was one other little wrinkle which was terribly interesting. American Express was not a corporation. It then was the only major publicly traded security that was a joint stock association. As such, the ownership of the company was assessable. If it turned out that the liabilities were greater than the assets, [then] the ownership was assessable. So every trust department in the United States panicked.

I remember the Continental Bank held over 5% of the company and all of a sudden not only do they see that the trust accounts were going to have stock worth zero, but it could get assessed. The stock just poured out, of course, and the market got slightly inefficient for a short period of time.

The American Express Company was a unique company to understand. You could look at that credit card and you knew it was a winner. Diner's Club had been the first, Carte Blanche had come along, but the American Express Card was killing them. They had raised prices every time. Their retention rate was higher. And finally, they raised prices, and Diner's Club didn't go along, and their growth far outstripped Diner's Club even though they were selling at a higher price. So this was a dynamite asset.

The traveler's check business had 60% of the traveler's check business in the world while selling their checks at a higher price than the banks, B of A and what was then First National Citibank, which were the two main competitions.

So here were two guys, B of A and First National City, undercutting them on price for 60 years and they still had 2/3 of the market. That is a moat around the business. I went out and did a little check to make sure this thing wasn't affecting them and we bought 5% of the American Express Company for $20 million, which means the whole company was selling for about $150 million at that time.

The whole American Express Company, synonymous with financial integrity and money substitutes around the world. When they closed the banks, when Roosevelt closed the banks, he exempted American Express Traveler's Checks, so they substituted as US currency.

It was not a business that should have been selling for $150 million, but everyone was terrified. It was very hard to tell how it would all come out in the end. But, probably, it was going to be between $60 and $100 million, and that was a lot more money back then in '62 than it is now. I just took the attitude that they'd declared a dividend of $75 million, sent it out and it got lost. Would that have caused a panic – somebody else gets your dividend but you don't.

No one would have argued about the value of American Express. They just didn't want to own it for a while. That's what you're buying periodically. They didn't want to own the Washington Post in '74. All you've got to do is find one, two or three businesses like that in a lifetime, load up when you do, and not do anything in between. There will be bigger whales in the ocean and they'll (garbled). There will be more of those as we go along. It's harder when you're working with more money, but there'll always be something.

[Question from audience: How many really good stock investments do you think are out there?]

Well, I would say this. If we were working with $25 million – so we could sort of look at the whole universe of stocks – I would guess that you could find 15 or 20 out of three or four thousand that you would find that were A) selling for substantially less than they're worth, and B) that the intrinsic value of the business was going to grow at a compound rate which was very satisfactory.

You don't want to buy a dollar bill that's sitting for 50 cents, and it demands positive capital, and it's going to be a dollar bill ten years from now. You want a dollar bill that's going to compound at 12% for [a long time]. And, you want to be around some competent people. Just the same thing as if you went in and bought a Ford dealership in South Bend.

The same exact thought processes goes through you mind if some friend called you tonight and said, "I'd like you to go into the Ford dealership" or whatever, is exactly the kind of thought as goes through mind about all the other businesses that are in Standard and Poor's.

When I was 20, I went through Moody's and Standard and Poor's page by page – twice – because that is it, that's the universe. The universe is much smaller now, unfortunately.

I found some strange things when I was 20 years old. I went through Moody's Bank and Finance Manual, about 1,000 pages. I went through it twice. The first time I went through, I saw a company called Western Insurance Security Company in Fort Scott, Kansas. They owned 92%, at that time, of the Western Casualty and Surety Company. Perfectly sound company. I knew people that represented them in Omaha. Earnings per share $20, stock price $16. (garbled) ... much more than that. I ran ads in the Fort Scott, Kansas paper to try and buy that stock – it had only 300 or 400 shareholders. It was selling at one times earnings. It had a first class [management team]...

...Incidentally, I would say that almost everybody I know in Wall Street has had as many good ideas as I have; they just had a lot of [bad] ideas, too. And I'm serious about that. I mean when I bought Western Insurance Security selling at $16 and earning $20 per share, I put half my net worth into it. I checked it out first – I went down to the insurance commission and got out the convention statements, I read Best's, and I did a lot of things first. But, I mean, my dad wasn't in it, I'd only had one insurance class at Columbia – but it was not beyond my capabilities to do that, and it isn't beyond your capabilities.

Now if I had some rare insight about software, or something like that – I would say that, maybe, other people couldn't do that – or biotechnology, or something. And I'm not saying that every insight that I have is an insight that somebody else could have, but there were all kinds of people that could have understood American Express Company as well as I understood it in '62. They may have been...they may have had a different temperament than I did, so that they were paralyzed by fear, or that they wanted the crowd to be with them, or something like that, but I didn't know anything about credit cards that they didn't know, or about travelers checks. Those are not hard products to understand.

But what I did have was an intense interest and I was willing, when I saw something I wanted to do, to do it. And if I couldn't see something to do, to not do anything. By far, the most important quality is not how much IQ you've got. IQ is not the scarce factor. You need a reasonable amount of intelligence, but the *temperament* is 90% of it.

That's why Graham is so important. Graham's book [*The Intelligent Investor*] talks about the qualities of temperament you have to bring to the game, and that is the game. Now I can (garbled).

He may not know anything about a Coca Cola, or something of

that sort, but that isn't what makes you the money. What makes you the money is your attitude going in, your attitude toward stock market fluctuations. There's two chapters in *The Intelligent Investor*, chapter 8 and chapter 20, they're more important than everything that's been written on investments, in my view, before or since. And there's no specific technical knowledge in those things.

It just tells you what frame of mind to be in when you come to the game. And people just don't get it. But that is not because I'm particularly skillful. And bear in mind that I didn't have that (garbled). It's not like I was Mozart and sat down at five or something. I mean I was churning things, I was computing odd lot statistics, I mean I loved all that stuff because I always liked numbers and playing around with them. It was like baseball averages or something. But what I needed was a philosophical bedrock position from which I could then go out and look at businesses, and probe through that filter, and decide whether that's [a bargain or not]. And that's Ben Graham's contribution. And that's the game. You don't have to be that smart. You don't have to know advanced accounting. It may *help* if you know something, particularly accounting. But the fact that you don't know it may restrict your universe some.

[Garbled comment from audience]

It goes back to a debate I was having with Mike Jensen [a proponent of the efficient market theory who famously wrote in 1978 that, "There is no other proposition in economics which has more solid empirical evidence supporting it than the Efficient Market Hypothesis"]. [I rebutted the efficient market hypothesis in] *The [Super] Investors of Graham and Doddsville*. It was an address I gave on the 50th anniversary of *Security Analysis*. Dave Dodd was there – 90 years old, marvelous guy.

And in that room were a half a dozen or more of us who had gone on to study or work, or have some association with Ben Graham. We weren't all five-sigma types, but we've always gotten five-sigma, or three-sigma, or something results. So it isn't because he had carefully culled us out from all over the country, like the Notre Dame football team. We were there just because we kind of stumbled in.

And we listened to the guy and then went out and applied it in different ways – totally different ways. I mean, Walter Schloss [has always] owned hundreds of different stocks. Walter is not a 150 IQ guy. Charlie Munger is. There were all different types of [people] with a common philosophical bond. They did not learn any little secrets of technique – they did not learn any systems.

Everybody wants a system. I mean they come to our annual meeting (garbled) the book guy, or the price/earnings, "Do I buy them on Monday?" They all want some [system] that you can run through a computer and simulate it out. I mean, I tell 'em if past performance were the key to it, the Forbes 400 would consist of librarians. Everybody would be looking it up. It doesn't work that way. They *want* it to work that way.

It would be so nice if it did, but it is not that way. It's like picking out a basketball team. You look for guys who are seven feet tall, you look for a guy who can stay in school; there are a whole bunch of things. And there are certain things that point you toward getting the best five guys out there on the court. But I can't give them a formula.

I can't say, "Here's a little formula and if you go to Emporia, Kansas and apply this formula without actually seeing the guys play basketball and working with them, you'll pick up the best basketball team." You won't.

[Question from audience: What is your opinion of today's investment teachings?]

To me, it's absolutely fascinating that the teaching of investments has really retrogressed from 40 years ago, and I think it's probably because the teachers are more skillful. They learn all these huge mathematical techniques and (garbled) and they have so much fun manipulating numbers they're missing something very simple.

And I think they have, on balance (aside: I say this at Stanford or Harvard), sent people off with the wrong message. And I get letters from students about it. I don't see what the reason for having an investment course is unless you teach people how to analyze the value of investments.

If people thought there was nothing of utility that you could impart on the subject, except for the fact that there is nothing you can do useful, then I don't understand... And I know it isn't true because I've seen people teach other people how to make unusual returns over a 30- or 40-year T-Note.

Phil Caret wrote a book on investing in 1924. He's still alive, he's a shareholder of Berkshire, he's 92 or 93 years old. He writes me letters that say, "I approve of your no dividend policy because when I get older, then I want to start getting dividends." But Phil Caret has got a record of 70 years.

That is a *lot* of investments and it is a superior investment record. Not done exactly the same as Graham, but it's the same general approach. Even Keynes came to that view. He started out as a market timer. But in the '30s he [changed approaches]. [Keynes later said: "As time goes on, I get more and more convinced that the right method in investment is to put fairly large sums into enterprises which one thinks one knows something about."]

You can't teach people a formula. You can't come in at the start of the term, and when they get all through, understand E=MC squared. It's not like teaching geometry or something.

You shouldn't buy a stock, in my view, for any other reason than the fact that you think it's selling for less than it's worth, considering all the factors about the business.

I used to tell the stock exchange people that before a person bought 100 shares of General Motors they should have to write out on a [piece of paper:] "I'm buying 100 shares of General Motors at X" and multiply that by the number of shares "and therefore General Motors is worth more than $32 billion" or whatever it multiplies out to, "because ... [fill in the reasons]" And if they couldn't answer that question, their order wouldn't be accepted.

That test *should be applied*. I should never buy anything unless I can fill out that piece of paper. I may be wrong, but I would know the answer to that. "I'm buying Coca Cola right now, 660 million shares of stock, a little under $50. The whole company costs me about $32 billion dollars." Before you buy 100 shares of stock at $48 you ought to be able to answer, "I'm paying $32 billion today for the Coca Cola Company because..." [Banging the podium for emphasis.] If you can't answer that question, you shouldn't buy it. If you *can* answer that question, and you do it a few times, you'll make a lot of money.

[From the audience: Well, you bought it, how did you answer it?]

Well, it was only $14 billion. I would say this: "If you added a penny to price of every Coca Cola sold in the world this year, that would add $2 billion to pretax earnings." Now you tell me whether you think there's a penny, worldwide, of price flexibility per serving of Coke. Well, the answer is, "You *know* there is."

When they bought the Coca Cola Company, the Candler family bought it from Pembertons back in 1904 or 1906; they paid $2,000 for the company. If the Pemberton family had reserved a penny a serving royalty a serving, the Coca Cola company would be sending $2 *billion* to the Pemberton family every year and you wouldn't even see the difference in the figures. It's there.

Now that's not true when I was selling [men's suit] linings [Berkshire Hathaway's original business]. I sold men's suit linings for 20 years. We tried to raise our price a half a cent a yard, and on an 80-cent-a-yard product, people who'd done business with us for 80 years slammed the door in our face. (garbled) ..."but half a cent a yard"... Nobody ever went into a store and said "I'd like to buy a pinstripe suit with a Hathaway lining." Never. They say, "I want a coat," all over the world.

Now in this country, Pepsi is, unfortunately, more or less coexistent with Coke. This is their weakest market. They make more in Japan, with less than half the people and way less per capita usage than they make in the United States. Around the world a guy says, "I'll sell you an unmarked cola a penny cheaper"... It isn't going to happen. That is the fastest test.

A couple of fast tests about how good a business is. First question is, "How long does the management have to think before they decide to raise prices?" You're looking at marvelous business when you look in the mirror and say, "Mirror, mirror on the wall, how much should I charge for Coke this fall?"

[And the mirror replies, "More."] That's a great business. When you say, like we used to in the textile business, when you get down on your knees, call in all the priests, rabbis, and everyone else, [and say] "just another half cent a yard." Then you get up and they say, "We won't pay it." It's just night and day. I mean, if you walk into a drugstore, and you say, "I'd like a Hershey bar" and the man says, "I don't have any Hershey bars, but I've got this unmarked chocolate bar, and it's a nickel cheaper than a Hershey bar," you just go across the street and buy a Hershey bar. *That* is a good business.

The ability to raise prices – the ability to differentiate yourself in a real way, and a real way means you can charge a different price – *that* makes a great business.

I'll try this on the students later: What's the highest price of a daily newspaper in the United States? [Pause] The highest priced daily newspaper in the United States is the *Daily Racing Form*. 150,000 copies a day, $2.25 a copy, they go up in 25-cent intervals, and it doesn't affect circulation at all. Why? There is no substitute. If you go to the track, assuming you're a forms player, you don't want "Joe's Little Green Sheet", you want *The Form*. And it doesn't make any difference what it costs! There is no substitute. And that's why they've got a 65% pretax margin. It doesn't take a genius to figure it out.

There are products like that, and there are products like sheet steel. And they're night and day.

[From Audience: You said you only had to have a couple of good ideas. We at Notre Dame had a good one in having you here.] [Applause]

Lecture to MBA Students

I'll talk for a few minutes on some of the things that relate to this handout I've got, so if everybody has one, or looks with their neighbor, we'll get the (garbled) about how to make a lot of money in stocks as we go along.

Eddie Cantor had a problem with Goldman Sachs in the late '20s. [Cantor was a popular entertainer who lost his fortune in the crash.] He did not do very well in something he bought from them, so he worked them into his routine when he performed, and he told (garbled).

You know, Wall Street is a place that people drive to in Rolls Royces to get advice from people who ride to work on the subway.

I'd like to talk to you for just a few minutes about what I regard as the most important thing in investments and also in terms of your career. Because in your career what train you get on makes a lot of difference. Because frequently, perhaps generally, when people get out of business school, they don't give enough thought to exactly what sort of train they're going to get on. And it makes a tremendous difference whether you get involved in a prosperous company, one that's going to really do well. On balance, you want to go with a company whose stock is going to be a good investment over the years because there's going to be much more opportunity, there's going to be more money made, you're going to (garbled). And if you get involved with some of the businesses I've been involved with like trading stamps (garbled).

[Buffett is warning students to stay away from declining businesses such as Blue Chip Stamps, though this was in fact a highly successful investment. In the book *Damn Right!*, Janet Lowe wrote: "During the late 1960s and early 1970s, Munger, Guerin and Buffett gradually acquired a controlling interest in Blue Chip Stamps. This small company issued trading stamps, which merchants distributed. Customers collected and redeemed the stamps for merchandise. The investors saw untapped potential in the company's float account – the difference between stamps issued and stamps redeemed. Using this pool of capital, Blue Chip's controlling investors acquired several other companies: Wesco Financial, See's Candies and The Buffalo Evening News."]

It does make a difference what kind of a business you get associated with. For that reason I've set forth in this little handout Company A and Company E. I'm not going to tell you for the moment what these companies are. I'm going to tell you one thing about the two companies.

One of the companies, to the point of where this cuts off, lost its investors more money than virtually any business in the world. The other company made its owner more money than virtually any company in the world. So one of these two companies, Company A and Company E, has made one of its owners one of the five wealthiest people in the world, while the other company made its owners appreciably poorer, probably more so than any other company to that point in time.

Now I'll tell you a little bit about these companies (we're leading up to the question of whether the business makes a difference). Company A had thousands of MBAs working for it. Company E had none. I wanted to get your attention. Company A had all kinds of employee benefit programs, stock options, pensions, the works. Company E never had stock options. Company A had thousands of patents – they probably held more patents than just about any company in the United States. Company E never invented anything. Company A's product improved dramatically in this period, Company E's product just sat.

So far, based on what I've told you, does anybody have any idea of which company was the great success, and why? If you get to buy one of these two companies, and this is all you know, and you get to ask me one question to decide on which one to buy. If you ask me the right question, you will probably make the right decision about the company's stock, and one will make you enormously wealthy.

[Question from audience: What products does each company make?]

Both companies make products used every day. They started as necessities, highly useful, nothing esoteric about either one, although company A does have all these patents. There's more technology involved in company A.

[Question from audience: How many companies compete with either one?]

Good question, very good question. In effect, neither company had any competition. And that might differentiate in some cases.

Well, I'll tell you a little more about it. Company A is known as company A because it was in agony, and Company E, as Company E, because it was in ecstasy. Company A is American Telephone and Telegraph. I've omitted eight zeros on the left hand side, and the American Telephone and Telegraph Company, at the end of 1979, was selling for $10 billion less than the shareholders had either put in or left in the business. In other words, if shareholder's equity was "X" the market value was X minus $10 billion. So the money that shareholders had put in or left in the business had shrunk by $10 billion in terms of market value.

Company E, the excellent company, I left off only six zeros. And that happens to be a company called Thompson Newspapers. Thomson Newspapers, which most of you have probably never heard of, actually owns about 5% of the newspapers in the United States. But they're all small ones.

And, as I said, it has no MBAs, no stock options – still doesn't – and it made its owner, Lord Thompson. He wasn't Lord Thompson when he started – he started with 1,500 bucks in North Bay, Ontario buying a little radio station but, when he got to be one of the five richest men, he became Lord Thompson. I met him one time in England as a matter of fact, in 1972, and went up to see him. He'd never heard of me, but he was a very important guy. (I'd heard of him!)

I said, "Lord Thompson, you own the newspaper in Council Bluffs, Iowa. Council Bluffs is right across the river from Omaha, where I live, four or five miles from my house. I said, "Lord Thompson, You own the Council Bluffs [Daily Nonpareil?]. I don't suppose you'd ever think of selling it?" He said, "I wouldn't think of it." I said, "Lord Thompson, you've bought this paper in Council Bluffs, and you've never seen the paper, never seen the town, but I do notice that every year you raise prices." (garbled)

He's got the only way to talk to people – his was the only "megaphone" for merchants to announce commercial news in Council Bluffs. He said, "I figured that out before you did."

I said, "If you ever raise prices to the point where it's counterproductive (garbled)."

Then [I said], "I've got only one other question: How do you figure out how much to charge people? You look like a man of awesome commercial instincts – you started with a $1,500 radio station, now you're worth $4 or $5 billion dollars."

He said, "Well, that's another good question. I just tell my US managers to try and make 45% pretax and figure that's not gouging." And as I got to the elevator, he said, "If you ever hear of a newspaper you don't want to buy, call me. Collect."

I rode down and that was two years of business school. I mean, try to make 45% and call me collect if you ever find a paper you don't want to buy.

The telephone company, with the patents, the MBAs, the stock options, and everything else, had one problem, and that problem is illustrated by those figures on that lower left hand column. And those figures show the plant investment in the telephone business. That's $47 billion, starting off with, growing to $99 billion over an eight or nine year period. More and more and more money had to be tossed in, in order to make these increased earnings, going from $2.2 billion to $5.6 billion.

So, they got more money, but you can get more money from a savings account if you keep adding money to it every year. The progress in earnings that the telephone company made was only achievable because they kept on shoving more money into the savings account and the truth was, under the conditions of the '70s, they were not getting paid commensurate with the amount of money that they had to shove into the pot, whereas Lord Thompson, once he bought the paper in Council Bluffs, never put another dime in. They just mailed money every year. And as they got more money, he bought more newspapers. And, in fact, he said it was going to say on his tombstone that he bought newspapers in order to make more money in order to buy more newspapers [and so on].

The idea was that, essentially, he raised prices and raised earnings there every year without having to put more capital into the business.

One is a marvelous, absolutely sensational business; the other one is a terrible business. If you have a choice between going to work for a wonderful business that is not capital intensive, and one that is capital intensive, I suggest that you look at the one that is not capital intensive. I took 25 years to figure that out, incidentally.

On the next page, I've got a couple of other businesses here. Company E is the ecstasy on the left. You can see earnings went up nicely: they went from $4 million to $27 million. They only employed assets of $17 million, so that is really a wonderful business. On $17 million they earned $27 million, 150% on invested capital. That is a good business. The one on the right, Company A, the agony, had $11 or $12 million tied up, and some years made a few bucks, and in some years lost a few bucks.

Now, here again we might ask ourselves, "What differentiates these companies?" Does anybody have any idea why company E might have done so much better than Company A? Usually somebody says at this point, "Maybe company E was better managed than company A." There's only one problem with that conclusion and that is, Company E and Company A had the same manager – me!

The company E is our candy business, See's Candies out in California. I don't know how many of you come from the west, but it dominates the boxed chocolate business out there and the earnings went from $4 million to $27 million, and in the year that just ended they were about $38 million. In other words, they mail us all the money they make every year and they keep growing, and making more money, and everybody's very happy.

Company A was our textile business. That's a business that took me 22 years to figure out it wasn't very good. Well, in the textile business, we made over half of the men's suit linings in the United States. If you wore a men's suit, chances were that it had a Hathaway lining. And we made them during World War II, when customers couldn't get their linings from other people. Sears Roebuck voted us "Supplier of the Year." They were wild about us. The thing was, they wouldn't give us another half a cent a yard because nobody had ever gone into a men's clothing store and asked for a pin striped suit with a Hathaway lining. You just don't see that.

As a practical matter, if some guy's going to offer them a lining for 79 cents, [it makes no difference] who's going to take them fishing, and supplied them during World War II, and was personal friends with the Chairman of Sears. Because we charged 79½ cents a yard, it was "no dice."

See's Candies, on the other hand, made something that people had an emotional attraction to, and a physical attraction you might say. We're almost to Valentine's Day, so can you imagine going to your wife or sweetheart, handing her a box of candy and saying, "Honey, I took the low bid."

Essentially, every year for 19 years I've raised the price of candy on December 26. And 19 years goes by and everyone keeps buying candy. Every *ten* years I tried to raise the price of linings a fraction of a cent, and they'd throw the linings back at me. Our linings were just as good as our candies. It was much harder to run the linings factory than it was to run the candy company. The problem is, just because a business is lousy doesn't mean it isn't difficult.

In the end, I like to think anyway that if Alfred P. Sloan [the legendary CEO of General Motors during its heyday] came back and tried to run the lining business, it wouldn't make as much money as a good business. The product was undifferentiated. The candy product is differentiated. (Garbled story of Hershey Bar and Coke versus unbranded but modestly cheaper products).

You really want something where, if they don't have it in stock, you want to go across the street to get it. Nobody cares what kind of steel goes into a car. Have you ever gone into a car dealership to buy a Cadillac and said, "I'd like a Cadillac with steel that came from the South Works of US Steel." It just doesn't work that way, so that when General Motors buys they call in all the steel companies and say, "Here's the best price we've got so far, and you've got to decide if you want to beat their price, or have your plant sit idle."

I put one business in here, CBS versus Cap Cities in 1957, when my friend Tom Murphy took over Cap Cities. They had a little bankrupt UHF station in Albany. They ran it out of a home for retired nuns. And it was very appropriate because they had to pray every day. At that time CBS was the largest advertising medium in the world: $385 million in revenues whereas Cap Cities had $900,000 in revenues. Cap Cities made $37,000 a year and they paid my friend Murph $12,000 a year. CBS made $48 million pretax. Cap Cities was selling for $5 million in the market and priced on the come, while CBS was selling for $500 million.

Now, if you look at the two companies, Cap Cities has a market value of about $7 billion and CBS has a market value of about $2 billion. They were both in the same business, broadcasting. Neither one had, certainly Cap Cities didn't have, any patents. Cap Cities didn't have anything that CBS didn't have. And somehow CBS took a wonderful business that was worth $500 million, and over about 30 years they managed a little increase – peanuts – while my friend Murphy, with exactly the same business, with one little tiny UHF station in Albany, (bear in mind that CBS had the largest stations in New York City and Chicago) and my friend Murph just killed them. And you say, "How can that happen?" And that's what you ought to study in business school. You ought to study Tom Murphy at Cap Cities. And you also ought to study Bill Paley [who was the CEO] at CBS.

We have a saying around Berkshire that, "All we ever want to know is where we're going to die, so we'll never go there." And CBS is what you don't want. It's as important not to do what CBS did, and it is important to do what Cap Cities did. Cap Cities did a lot of things right, but if CBS had done the same things right, Cap Cities would have never come close.

They had all the IQ at CBS that they had at Cap Cities. They had 50 times as many people, and they were all coming to work early and going home late. They had all kinds of strategic planners. They had management consultants. They had more than I can say. Yet they *lost*. They lost to a guy that started out with a leaky rowboat, at the same time the other guy left in the QE II. By the time they got into New York, the guy in the rowboat brought in more cargo than the QE II did. There's a real story in that. And you can understand broadcasting, so it's really worth studying what two people in the same field did, and why one succeeded so much and one failed.

I couldn't resist kicking in the last page: the only public offering Cap Cities ever made, back in 1957 which raised, as you can see, $300,000. And this was when they were going to buy the station in Raleigh/Durham. The only public offering of stock the company's every made (aside: they sold us a block of stock when they bought ABC). And if you look very carefully you'll see that the underwriting commission – they took two firms to get this sold – the total underwriting commission was $6,500 bucks.

The last thing I want to show you, before we get onto your questions, is an ad that was run June 16, 1969, for 1,000,000 shares of American Motors. This is a reproduction from the *Wall Street Journal* of that day. Now does anybody notice anything unusual about that ad?

[Guesses from audience.]

Everybody in that ad has disappeared. There are 37 investment bankers that sold that issue, plus American Motors, and they are *all* gone. Maybe that's why they call them tombstone ads. Now the average business of the New York Stock exchange in 1969 was 11 million shares. Average volume now is *fifteen* times as large. Now here's an industry whose volume has grown 15 to 1 in 20 years. Marvelous growth in the financial world. And here are

72

37 out of 37, and those are some of the biggest names on Wall Street, and some of them had been around the longest, and 37 out of 37 have disappeared. And that's why I say you ought to think about [the long-term durability of a business?] because these people obviously didn't.

These were run by people with high IQs, by people that worked ungodly hard. They were people that had an intense interest in success. They worked long hours. They *all* thought they were going to be leaders on Wall Street at some point, and they all went around, incidentally, giving advice to other companies about how to run their business. That's sort of interesting. You go to Wall Street today, and there's some company the guy hadn't heard of two weeks before and he's trying to sell you. He will lay out this computer run of the next 10 years, yet he doesn't have the faintest idea of what his own business is going to earn next week!

Here are a group of 37. And the question is, how can you get a result like that? That is not a result that you get by chance. How can people who are bright, who work hard, who have their own money in the business – these are not a bunch of absentee owners – how can they get such a bad result? And I suggest that's a good thing to think about before you get a job and go out into the world.

I would say that if you had to pick one thing that did it more than anything else, it's the mindless imitation of one's peers that produced this result. Whatever the other guy did, the other 36 were like a bunch of lemmings in terms of following. That's what's gotten all the big banks in trouble for the past 15 years. Every time somebody big does something dumb, other people can hardly wait to copy it. If you do nothing else when you get out of here, do things *only* when they make sense to you. You ought to be able to write "I am going to work for General Motors because..." "I am buying 100 shares of Coca Coals stock because..." And if you can't write an intelligent answer to those questions, don't do it.

I proposed this to the stock exchange some years ago: that everybody be able to write out, "I am buying 100 shares of Coca Cola Company, market value $32 billion, because...." and they wouldn't take your order until you filled that thing out.

I find this very useful when I write my annual report. I learn while I think when I write it out. Some of the things I think I think, I find don't make any sense when I start tying to write them down and explain them to people. You ought to be able to explain why you're taking the job you're taking, why you're making the investment you're making, or whatever it may be. And if it can't stand applying pencil to paper, you'd better think it through some more.

People in that ad did a lot of things that could not have stood that test. Some *major* bankers in the United States did a lot of things that could not meet that test. One of the bankers in the United States, who's in plenty of trouble now, bragged a few years ago he never made a loan. And, from the way things are starting to look, he's never going to collect on one either.

You should not be running one the major banks in the United States without having made loans. I mean, you learn about human nature, if nothing else, when you make loans.

[Question and Answer With Students]

That jewelry store, it's an interesting story. I'll take an extra minute. We bought a furniture store about five or six years ago. We bought it from a woman who was 89 [Rose Blumkin, the legendary Mrs. B]. That woman came to this country with a tag around her neck from Russia. She walked out of Russia, and the Red Cross truck got her in Seattle and (garbled) then Fort Dodge, Iowa and sent her there. And she saved money. She sold used clothes and that sort of thing, and she brought over seven siblings, plus her mother and father. She sent over $50 bucks at a time to get the rest of the family over here.

In 1937, she would have been 44 at the time; she started a store with $500, a home furnishings store. That's all the money she ever put into it. Last year it made $18 million, pretax. It's become the largest home furnishings store in the country. And she put everybody out of business. She doesn't know accounting, she's never had an audit, she doesn't know what accruals mean, she doesn't know what depreciation means, but she knows how to run a business. And, unfortunately, two years ago she got mad at her grandchildren and she went out and quit and started competing with us, which shows you how stupid I was not to get a non-compete agreement from an 89-year-old woman! She is now in business right across the street, and works seven days a week at 97 years of age. And if you tell her that this room is 27 by 31, she will tell you how many square yards it is just like that, at $6.99 a yard, and how much that comes to plus tax. She can do it just like that. She cannot read or write. She has never been to school a day in her life. But she knows how to run a business.

One of the sisters she brought over, also to Omaha, was a woman named Rebecca. She went through Latvia, and the border guard took the money when she got to Latvia, and she had to sit in Latvia for a year until her sister got another $50 bucks to bring her over here. They got over here, and it took them 20 odd years to get enough money to buy into a tiny little jewelry store. And I bought that business a couple of years ago from the Friedman family, which is Mrs. B's sister. Incidentally, Mrs. B is 97, and her three other (garbled).

In any event, in that jewelry store last year, the sales were up 18%. I believe it's the second largest jewelry store in the United States, next to Tiffany's main location, and it uses *exactly* the same formula the furniture store used in building up the largest home furnishings store. The people that run them never went to business school, and they stress the things that Ben Franklin would stress. Essentially, their business is pure Ben Franklin. Tell truth and give people service. Ben Franklin said, "Take care of thy shop and it will take care of thee." Now that's old fashioned in terms of the phraseology, but it's that simple. And, the truth is that family... If you were at our jewelry store last Saturday like I was, Ike Friedman who is 65, 66, was there. His mother, Mrs. Friedman, came in – she's 89 years old – *Wall Street Journal* under her arm. You've got his son there, his only son, two sons-in-law, two daughters in there. They're all busy. The family's worth tens and tens and tens of millions of dollars. They don't do it 'cause they have to, they do it 'cause they like to.

The one thing we've done well in buying businesses is the people who sold them were in love with their business and not in love with money. If they're in love with money we can't do it, but if they're in love with their business we get along very well because we leave them alone.

Actually Fran Blumkin, the wife of Louis Blumkin, who's now Chairman of the Furniture Mart, comes in on Saturday, and works Tuesday, to help out Louis' cousins. And she sells jewelry all the time there. It's a great business. Berkshire bought a great business. It gets better, and better, and better. And *no one* can knock 'em off.

That's one of the things I always ask myself: If you give someone hundreds of millions of dollars, or billions of dollars, [can you hurt a particular business?] You can't hurt the Furniture Mart or Borsheim's.

[Question: When you look at a company, how do you value it, how do you decide how much to pay for it, and after that, would you say how much you'd sell it for?]

Well, we won't sell it. We just don't sell businesses. If we had a business that would permanently lose money, or we had a manager lie to us, or cheat us, or (garbled). But we will never sell a business just because we get a wonderful offer for it. My house isn't for sale. The children aren't for sale. The businesses aren't for sale. I tell shareholders that. That may make me crazy, but that's who they're getting in with, and they might as well know it. It is not a game we're playing, like gin rummy, where we pick up one card and discard another.

And I think good human relationships...I work with nothing but people I like. There's not one person I work with that causes my stomach to churn in the least. In fact, I feel like tap dancing. I work with nothing but people I like. Well, just think how fortunate you are if you're 60 years of age and that's the way you're going to be able to spend your life. These people are wonderful to work with. I mean, Ike Friedman...we never disagree. Charlie Munger, my partner, and I have never had a disagreement in 30 years. And, why in the world [would I sell businesses run by people I like] so that I can be worth 110% of X, instead of X, when I die? It will all be in the foundation anyway. Why should I go around discarding people like that who are in the business, for some people who might not turn out so well? So I'm not interested in selling at all.

Now, in terms of buying, a) I've got to like the people. I'm just not interested in marrying for money. That might have been great when I was 12, but it would be crazy now for me to marry someone for money. Why should I marry in business for money? It just doesn't make sense. I get associated with these people, so I want to buy the people I like, and I want to buy businesses I understand, and then I don't want to think too much. And, paying too much simply comes out.

If you can tell me what all of the cash in and cash out of a business will be, between now and judgment day, I can tell you, assuming I know the proper interest rate, what it's worth. It doesn't make any difference whether you sell yo-yo's, hula hoops, or computers. Because there would be a stream of cash between now and judgment day, and the cash spends the same, no matter where it comes from. Now my job as an investment analyst, or a business analyst, is to figure out where I may have some knowledge, what that stream of cash will be over a period of time, and also where I don't know what the stream of cash will be. I don't have the faintest idea of where Digital Equipment will be in next week, let alone the next 10 years. I just don't know. I don't even know what they do. And I never would know what they did. Even if I thought I knew what they did, I wouldn't know what they did. Hershey bars I understand.

So, my job is to look at the universe of things I can understand – I can understand Ike Friedman's jewelry store – and then I try to figure what that stream of cash, in and out, is going to be over a period of time, just like we did with See's Candies, and discounting that back at an appropriate rate, which would be the long term Government rate. [Then,] I try to buy it at a price that is significantly below that. And that's about it. Theoretically, I'm doing that with all the businesses in the world – those that I can understand.

Every day, when I turn to the *Wall Street Journal*, back in the C Section, that's like a big business brokerage ad. It's just like a business broker saying, "You can buy part of AT&T for this, part of General Motors for that, General Electric..." And unlike most business broker's ads, it's nice because they change the price every day. And you don't have to do business with any of them. So you just sit there, day by day, and you yawn, and you insult the broker if you want to, and talk to your newspaper, anything you want to, because someday, there's going to be some business I understand selling for way less than the value I arrived at. It doesn't have anything to do with book value, although it does have to do with earnings power over a period of time. It usually relates, fairly closely, to cash [flow]. And, when you find something you understand, if you find five ideas in your lifetime and you're right on those five, you're going to be very rich.

You know, I always tell business students that if you got a punch card when you got out of here, and it only had 20 businesses on it, and every time you made an investment decision they took a punch, and when the 20 were gone you were all done, it would be wonderful. You're not going to get more than 20 investment ideas in a lifetime. I'm not going to get more than 20 great ideas.

And the important thing is that you recognize them when you see them, and that you do something about them.

So, when we find something we understand, if we're buying all of the business, I want to like the people. If we're buying part of the business, it's less important. We want to buy things we understand, and we want to buy them very cheap. If we don't understand them, we don't buy them. If they're not cheap, we don't buy them. If we can buy them with Tom Murphy, my friend, at an attractive price, we do that in a second.

We bought 5% of the Walt Disney Company in 1966. It cost us $4 million dollars; $80 million bucks was the valuation of the whole thing; 300 and some acres in Anaheim. The Pirate's ride had just been put in. It cost $17 million bucks. The whole company was selling for $80 million. Mary Poppins had just come out. Mary Poppins *made* about $30 million that year, and seven years later you're going to show it to kids the same age.

It's like having an oil well where all the oil seeps back in. Now the [numbers today are] probably different, but in 1966 they had 220 pictures of one sort or another. They wrote them all down to zero – there were no residual values placed on the value of any Disney picture up through the '60s. So [you got all of this] for $80 million bucks, and you got Walt Disney to work for you. It was incredible. You didn't have to be a genius to know that the Walt Disney Company was worth more than $80 million. Seventeen million dollars for the Pirate's Ride.

It's unbelievable. But there it was. And the reason was, in 1966 people said, "Well, Mary Poppins is terrific this year, but they're not going to have another Mary Poppins next year, so the earnings will be down." I don't care if the earnings are down like that. You know, you've still got Mary Poppins to throw out in seven more years, assuming kids squawk a little. I mean there's no better system than to have something where, essentially, you get a new crop every seven years and you get to charge more each time.

Eighty million dollars [sigh]. I went out to see Walt Disney (he'd never heard of me; I was 35 years old). We sat down and he told me the whole plan for the company – he couldn't have been a nicer guy. It was a joke. If he'd privately gone to some huge venture capitalist, or some major American corporation, if he'd been a private company, and said, "I want you to buy into this. This is a deal," they would have bought in based on a valuation of $300 or $400 million dollars. The very fact that it was just sitting there in the market every day convinced [people that $80 million was an appropriate valuation]. Essentially, they ignored it because it was so familiar. But that happens periodically on Wall Street.

I wanted to go see Mary Poppins, to see if she'd be recycled, and she was showing at the Loews Theater on 45th and Broadway in New York, and here I am with a briefcase at 2:00 in the afternoon heading in to see Mary Poppins. I almost felt like I had to rent a kid.

[Question from audience: What is the relationaship between Walt Disney and Salomon?]

There's very little relationship between Walt Disney and Salomon. In Salomon we have lent them, in effect, $700 million on a preferred, which matures in five equal installments, starting five years from now, which is also convertible. And this is primarily a fixed income investment with an interesting conversion privilege attached to it.

But it is not primarily an equity investment. We get a 9% dividend, which, because of the corporate dividend tax credit, converts to something over 7% on an after-tax basis. It's a form of lending money. It's an alternative to municipal bonds or something of that sort. It is *not* an investment like Coca Cola, or the Washington Post, or Cap Cities, which are pure equity investments.

We would rather, and this is nothing negative on Salomon, buy more things like Coca Cola. You know, those are the things that really cause excitement, because those are super businesses as far as the eye can see. Salomon is a perfectly decent business, but it's just not the same kind of business. Neither is Champion Paper or US Air, which we've done the same thing for. If we had way less money, we wouldn't be doing those things, as opposed to the Coca Cola thing. It's because we can't find more of those. And we should own some fixed income investments because of our [insurance business].

[Question from audience: How did you start out in the investing world?]

Well, I started out when I was 20. I had just finished Ben Graham's course. And I took Moody's Manuals – they had investment manuals – and I took Standard and Poor's, where they put them all together, and do them all alphabetically, and I went through them all page by page. And things jumped out at me.

I saw Western Insurance Services, in Fort Scott, Kansas, looking in Moody's Bank and Finance Manuals. I'd never heard of Western Insurance Services until I turned that page that said Western Insurance Services. It showed earnings per share of $20 and the high was $16. Now that may not turn out to be something you can make a lot of money on, but the odds are good. It's like a basketball coach seeing a guy 7'3" walk through the door. He may not be able to stay in school, and may be very uncoordinated, but he's very large.

So I went down to the Nebraska Insurance Department, and I got the convention reports on their insurance companies, and I read Best's. I didn't have any background in insurance. But I knew I could understand it if I worked at it for a while. And all I was really trying to do was disprove this thing. I was really trying to figure out something that was wrong with this. Only there wasn't anything wrong. It was a perfectly good insurance company, a better than average underwriter, and you could buy it at one times earnings. I ran ads in the Fort Scott, Kansas paper to buy this stock when it was $20. But it came through turning the pages. No one tells you about it. You get 'em by looking.

I read hundreds of annual reports every year. I don't talk to any brokers – I don't want to talk to brokers. People are not going to give you great ideas. On the other hand, getting them is not that difficult. If you'd read the Disney report in 1966, believe me, you'd have known as much about Disney then as now. You wouldn't have Michael Eisner, you'd have Walt Disney running it. And you could have multiplied, at two million shares outstanding (garbled).

Cap Cities at that time was an act of faith. You had to believe in Tom Murphy. You could not see (garbled).

(Garbled) and some of you will be stars, and some of you will be less than stars. But it won't correlate with your IQ at all. But you have it already. And everybody in the room has it. I'll give you a little question. Let's think about this. Let's say that everyone here got a bonus when they left Notre Dame. Let's say for $25,000 you could buy a 10% interest in the income of any one of your classmates that you wanted to. Now, what are you thinking about? You can take anybody in this room, and for $25,000 buy a 10% interest in their income for life. If they make $25,000 the first year, you make $2,500. If they're unemployed, you don't get anything. If they get stock options, you get 10% of the stock options. What are you thinking about as you look around? Are you thinking about which ones are the smartest? It's interesting what ingredients you think now are what's going to produce that in the classroom. I would suggest that you start thinking about, assuming you have a 10% interest, what qualities you want to have. I know I would take Tom Murphy. Why? Well, he's got an IQ, there's no question about that. But, that's something one or two others might have as well.

Think about why you picked him or her, and how much of that is transferable to you. And it usually won't be anything you can't attain yourself. But if it's qualities of character, or qualities of enthusiasm, or whatever it may be, most of those things you can pick up.

[Question from audience: When would you invest money from the company in the market?]

Well, we will do that anytime we feel that a dollar we retain in the company is not going to be worth more than a dollar in market price. And that can happen. I mean, as we get bigger, it's more likely to happen.

But so far, every dollar we've kept in the company has translated into more than a dollar in market price, so that anybody who wanted to take $10 a share out, or $50 a share out, is better off having us keep the $50, having at appraised in the market at $60, $70, or $80 and selling a little piece.

They actually come out dollars ahead by doing that. But, when we can't use the money for any extended period, not for a month or three months, but a period of years, when we find out that we don't have ways to use money in a way that creates more than a dollar of market value for each dollar reinvested, then we won't.

I couldn't attend the 50th birthday of one of my friends so I sent him a telegram: "May you live until Berkshire splits." That doesn't apply to cash dividends. It will be a market failure but, nevertheless, that may be what happens.

[Question from audience: Are Security Pacific and Wells Fargo headed for a merger?]

Well, I won't comment too much on that. The question is whether Security Pacific and Wells Fargo, two of the four largest banks in California, were in talks late last year, and a story appeared in the *Wall Street Journal* talking about this a week or two ago. They were in talks last year about merging. And that excited some people because Wells had done a particularly good job when they took over Crocker four years ago, or so.

And then the deal, the Security Pacific/Wells Fargo thing, did not happen. And then the story leaked out so it's in the paper. Security Pacific is probably an $80 billion bank. Wells Fargo, I know, is a $50 billion bank. It would have created what would have been the second largest bank in the country, next to Citicorp.

My guess is there will be some bank mergers in the next few years, but they may be more suicide pacts than mergers. There's going to be a lot of action, not all good by a long shot, in banks, simply because there's so much trouble there. The big problem in merging two banks these days is that you don't know what's in the other guy's loan portfolio – because too often *he* doesn't know. And people didn't used to worry about that five or 10 years ago, and they worry about it a whole lot now because, if they merge with the wrong bank, they can go broke.

C&S, the Citizens and Southern Bank of Atlanta, merged with Sovereign earlier this year. Sovereign has got a lot of real estate problems in the Washington D.C. area, and that merger took place less than 12 months ago.

Al Lerner merged his Equitable Trust Company in Baltimore into the old Maryland National. Al Lerner is a very, very, smart fellow. And he merged his own company, which he had a lot of his own money in, he merged it in with MNC and in six months MNC was in huge trouble.

The stock was 10% of what the value was when he merged it six months ago. And Al just got in with something where he didn't know how bad it was.

But that was easy to do. So, everybody is super careful about that, and this is why there's a problem, because to look at a Wells

Fargo with assets of $50 billion, and Security Pacific with $80 billion, and if there's $2 or $3 billion in there that's no good, that wipes out equity. That's a tough decision to make.

[Question from audience: How is the insurance business these days?]

Right now, in property/casualty insurance, generally speaking, prices are lousy, which means business is terrible. We have found a few things to do that will be in our annual report. We've found a few things that are OK, they're not like they were four or five years ago, but they're keeping us out of bars. And that's what we look for in times like this. But that is a *very* interesting business. When that guy was predicting an earthquake near New Madrid we wrote a two-month policy against a $3 billion earthquake for some crazy rate as a percentage of everything. We ought to keep that guy out there.

We've had a chance to do some very interesting things in insurance. It's a very tricky business. We are getting in claims on policies we wrote in 1970. We're not getting in any premium. We're just getting in claims. They tell the story in insurance...

[Told burying dad in a rented suit story. From the 2001 Berkshire Hathaway annual letter:

Even when companies have the best of intentions, it's not easy to reserve properly. I've told the story in the past about the fellow traveling abroad whose sister called to tell him that their dad had died. The brother replied that it was impossible for him to get home for the funeral; he volunteered, however, to shoulder its cost. Upon returning, the brother received a bill from the mortuary for $4,500, which he promptly paid. A month later, and a month after that also, he paid $10 pursuant to an add-on invoice. When a third $10 invoice came, he called his sister for an explanation. "Oh," she replied, "I forgot to tell you. We buried dad in a rented suit."

There are a lot of "rented suits" buried in the past operations of insurance companies. Sometimes the problems they signify lie dormant for decades, as was the case with asbestos liability, before virulently manifesting themselves. Difficult as the job may be, it's management's responsibility to adequately account for *all* possibilities. Conservatism is essential. When a claims manager walks into the CEO's office and says, "Guess what just happened," his boss, if a veteran, does not expect to hear it's good news. Surprises in the insurance world have been far from symmetrical in their effect on earnings.]

We literally will pay hundreds of thousand of dollars for things that happened years back. On the other hand, overall, it can be a good business if you're disciplined. We have a rule. We're very Japanese in that, we never lay off anybody. We tell them, in times like this where we're writing way less than we were writing a few years ago, we tell them that under no conditions will they be laid off for lack of business because otherwise they'll go out an write some business. I mean, it's the easiest thing in the world to do.

And we tell them we'll buy them golf memberships, country club memberships, if they'll promise to play golf during business hours, because we don't want them in the office during business under terms that are generally available these days. So we occasionally run into a good big deal, and we keep busy that way, but we are operating at 1/4 speed. We have a lot of people that are doing crossword puzzles, which is fine. It beats whatever else they'd be doing. You do not want energetic people in a lousy business.

[Question from audience: What business publications do you read?]

I read all kinds of business publications. I read a lot of industry publications. Coming in today on the plane (garbled). I'll grab whatever comes in the morning. American Banker comes every day, so I'll read that. I'll read the *Wall Street Journal*. Obviously. I'll read *Editor and Publisher*, I'll read *Broadcasting*, I'll read *Property Casualty Review*, I'll read *Jeffrey Meyer's Beverage Digest*. I'll read everything. And I own 100 shares of almost every stock I can think of just so I know I'll get all the reports. And I carry around prospectuses and proxy material. Don't read broker's reports. You should be very careful with those.

[Question from audience: Which of the publication do you think is the most important?]

I think the *Wall Street Journal* is essential. I spend 45 minutes a day with the *Wall Street Journal*. Actually, I got up the night before, about 11:00... I frequently read it at night. But I'll read anything. Actually, I probably spend five or six hours a day on reading.

We have no meetings at Berkshire. We have a directors meeting once a year, after the shareholders meeting, at lunch. And at the end, I say, "I'll see you next year." It's a very economical operation. We don't have a slide projector.

We don't have a calculator. We do not have meetings on anything. If I take Ike Friedman, and bring him to a meeting, I've probably lost $20,000 or something. He should be out there selling. There just isn't anything to meet about. He's having meetings in his head all the time about the jewelry store. I'm having meetings in my head about what to do with the money.

We don't attend any seminars, or trade things. I get all this stuff about how to incorporate in the Cayman Islands or how to never write a check to the IRS. We don't do any of that stuff. There's not much goes on at the place, and that's probably just as well. Every now and then we get a chance to do something and we do it as best as we can.

When Coca Cola got to where it was attractive, for seven or eight months we bought every share of Coca Cola we could. We bought what, on the old stock, 23 million shares, we probably bought that on 150 trading days, that's 160,000 shares a day. You've got to do it when the time is right to do it.

[Question from audience: Have you ever considerd buying any British companies?]

I look at them. I read the *Financial Times* every day. We've looked at, and we've come close, very close, to one deal. There's another proposition I've got right now from somebody. But so far, we haven't done anything. But I don't rule it out.

If Coca Cola were located in London, and was an English company, and did business exactly like they do, it would be worth slightly less than [if it were a US company]. But overall, I'd do it. Obviously.

We've looked at a lot [at foreign companies]. [But] we've got a $3 trillion pond in terms of market value in this country. And if I can't make money in a $3 trillion pond, I can't make money in an $8 trillion pond. We tend to look in the $3 trillion pond mostly.

[Question from audience: Is it a good idea for business owners to sell their businesses?]

Usually they won't. And I tell them, almost always, they shouldn't. I'm going to have a letter in the annual report this year which I've sent many times to possible sellers of businesses. And the one thing I tell them is you're not richer when you sell a business. You've got a wonderful asset that will be worth more money later on. I wouldn't be talking to you if I didn't think this was the case. If it takes care of a specific problem you have, and you want somebody that meets these certain parameters, we'll talk. If it doesn't, that's great. You've got something better than I've got, because I've got cash, and I've got a problem, and you've got a good business, and you don't have a problem.

Mrs. B wasn't richer when she sold me the business. She did have one son and, at that time, three grandsons in the business, and she had three daughters and their husbands, and a bunch of their children who weren't in the business, and everybody owned 20% of it. So she thought there would be some sort of problem when she died.

She was a strong enough matriarchal figure that there weren't and problems when she lived – she told them what to do, and that was it. But, when she was gone, she could see trouble. You saw it down at the Louisville Courier/Journal a couple of years ago with the Bingham family. You get a lot of money, but somebody gets unhappy.

Sometimes the in-laws get unhappy. Some people prefer to solve that problem themselves, when they're alive, rather than have some trust department try and solve it when they are dead. But, I don't want people selling to me because they think they're getting richer, I want them selling to me because it solves some particular problem, and I can help them solve it.

I can do things that other companies can't do. I can arrange the transfer of some of the ownership of the business to another generation. I can promise them it won't get resold. Virtually no other American company can do that. If the XYZ company goes out and buys See's or Borsheim's, the President of XYZ company can say, "We're not going to sell it," but he may be taken over himself, his board of directors may tell him to do something, McKinsey may come in next week and say, "Get out of this business and get into some other business." You can get double crossed in a lot of ways that there's no moral stigma attached to, but that's just the way the cards fall. With me, that can't happen.

The only thing that can happen bad to them is if I double cross them. So they have to make a judgment whether I'm lying to them. I can't come back to them later and say the board's told me we've got to get out of the jewelry business, there's this great offer that's come in, I've got this fiduciary responsibility, blah, blah, blah, blah. That won't happen.

[Question from audience: Do business owners get rich by selling to you?]

They're rich because they've already gotten rich by having the company. All they're going to do, if they take money from me, is they're going pay some taxes, and they're going to invest in some other business. They might buy Berkshire, they might buy General Motors, they might buy government bonds, but they already had a good business. And they don't have to pay the taxes. So they are not getting richer.

I can help them with some problems. When Ike at Borsheim's came to me I said, "Look, I will pay you X, and I will show you how to get more money than that, and here is how you can do it." He said, "I'm not interested."

We don't want what I call the used cigar butts, where you get one free puff and that's it. (garbled comment from audience). Well, partly I don't have the people to stick in anyway. And I don't want to go through the human travail that's involved in that.

I don't want to go through it, basically. And, if you have your choice, we'll just think in terms of looks now, but marrying some gal that's the girl of your dreams and having another one and saying, "If I send her to the psychotherapist for five years and have some plastic surgery," well, maybe it will work.

Lecture to Undergraduate Students

...we let the operating managers run their businesses, and we have them send the money to Omaha. And then we try to buy more businesses. And sometimes we can buy all of a business, and sometimes we can only buy part of it. But we're the largest shareholder of the Coca Cola Company, we're the largest shareholder of Capital Cities/ABC Broadcasting, we're the largest shareholder of Gillette Company, and then probably Champion Paper, Geico, the insurance company, the Wells Fargo bank. There's quite a few.

We buy entire businesses, or we buy tiny pieces of businesses called "stocks" and we have the same approach to it. And if the capital comes in, we're willing to do either one. In this year's annual report, in answer to the question of what I do, I tell the story of my granddaughter's birthday party...

[Told Beemer the Clown story again]

I sit there in Omaha and wave my magic wand. But, I've got all these Beemers out there, running businesses. They run them exceptionally well. Our businesses are generally characterized by unusual market strength and terrific continuity of management.

Almost everybody that works for us is independently rich because we've usually bought their business. And they've received a lot of money from us. And one of the main parts of my job is to figure out, when I'm sitting across the table from John Smith and I'm going to hand him a check for $50 or $100 million, I have to decide whether he's going to get out of bed the next morning. And it's very important to me that he is just as interested in running his business, and he thinks of it as his business, the next day, and the next year, and the next decade, as he was when he owned it all himself. With a lot of people, there's no way to buy that.

You can't set up an incentive compensation scheme that accomplishes that because they've already got all the money they need. You really have to make a judgment as to whether they run their business because they love business or because they love money. If they love money, we don't have a chance. We can pay them a lot of money, but they've already got a lot of money.

They never need to come to work another day in their life after they sell out to us, and yet virtually all of them work harder now than they've ever worked before. The main reason for this is that they're that type – that is the way they're put together.

Secondarily, we try to provide an environment for them, which is exactly like what we'd want if we were running a business. The main thing we would want is we would not want a lot of second guessing, we would not want a lot of home office meetings, we would not want a lot of supervision from some group Vice President at headquarters. We just would not want a lot of nonsense. We would like to run our own business in our own way. If you were a great golfer, and let's just say, going back to my generation, you were Arnold Palmer.

You'd basically play golf because you like to play golf. But if he was playing golf, and we were doing it for money, and in some way I owned him, and I kept saying, "Why don't you use a four iron instead of a five iron, and why don't you aim a littler further to the right?" After a while, he'd wrap the club around my neck, and rightly so. If you get really talented people, you've got to give them a chance to do their own thing.

We bought a uniform company in Cincinnati five years ago, a $100 million company. I've never been to Cincinnati. I've never seen a factory of theirs. I don't know what their offices look like. I know the people quite well.

We've got a candy company, See's Candies in California. We sold 13.5 million tons of boxed chocolates last year and made $39 million before taxes. The fellow that runs it has been running it from the day we bought it 19 years ago. We made a deal with him, and in 30 seconds worked out an incentive compensation agreement. In 30 seconds. Never wrote it down, never had a lawyer. That deal is still the same deal 19 years later. He's been to Omaha exactly once.

Last year he came to the annual meeting to see whether there really was a Berkshire Hathaway in Omaha. We've never had a group meeting of any kind. We don't force anything on them. We actually moved the headquarters of the company from Los Angeles to San Francisco because his wife liked living in San Francisco better than she like Los Angeles. Instead of having a guy with a wife that was considerably less happy living in LA, it was a lot easier to move the business to San Francisco, so that's where it comes from now.

We have no retirement age. We had a woman running a business for us, we'd bought her business when she was 89, and she was Chairman of the Board, and she ran it for us until she got mad two years ago and left at 95, because, foolishly, I'd forgotten to get a non-compete agreement from this 89-year-old woman when we made the deal.

She now competes with us across the street. She works seven days a week. We've never let anybody go because of age. We had one fellow, ran a savings and loan for us in Pasadena [Wesco Financial], he kept trying to get me to get somebody else. He was 75 years old. [He'd say], "You've got to get another guy in here," and I'd say, "Louis, how's your mother?" She lived to be 93 and that ended the conversation.

So we have a business with very few rules. The only rules the managers have is to basically think like owners. We want those people thinking exactly like they own those businesses themselves. Psychologically, we don't even want them to think there is a Berkshire Hathaway. They know they will never get sold. They don't have to sit around and wonder if there's going to be a takeover raid on Berkshire.

Let's talk a little bit about what you're interested in. This is a little bit different group than I usually talk to, its almost always been MBAs in the past, and its quite refreshing to get a mixture of liberal arts people in, so you can throw anything at me that you care to – nothing's off limits.

[Question from audience: Do business owners get rich by selling to you?]

They hardly get richer because they sell to me. I tell them, "If you come to me, and you've got a wonderful business, I can't make you richer than you are. If you sell to me for $100 million, it's only because your business is worth $100 million. And you'll pay a lot of taxes and you won't have $100 million. If you take the remainder after-tax and buy General Motors and AT&T you'll have a lot of businesses you don't understand, instead of one you do understand. There's no reason to sell to me to get richer. I always tell people the only reason I'm buying is because I think it's going to be worth more. If they are selling to me simply to stick a lot of money into their own pocket, it's the wrong reason.

One woman was 89 when she sold to me. She had four children. One worked in the business; three didn't work in the business. She had multitudes of grandchildren. Three of them worked in the business, two of them didn't. The stock was divided equally, 20% with each branch, plus 20% she kept. As long as she was around, she was an enormously strong personality, there weren't going to be any problems because she was going to tell people what he answers were.

The day she died, she felt that there would be a developing situation where people didn't work and wanted to get the money out of the business and that the people who did work would resent the fact that the people who didn't work were cashing in.

You get a lot of that as families move along. So she preferred to solve it herself by getting cash for the members of the family that weren't involved in the business, and then I moved the ownership of the remaining people down to the lowest generation of the ones that were in the business. That happens a variety of times.

The uniform company we own in Cincinnati had an LBO some years earlier and there were four or five venture capital firms there and they just wanted to take a quick profit. The guy who ran it realized he'd made a mistake when he sold out to a group like that in the first place, so he steered it to us. He wrote me out of the blue.

I've got a little ad in my annual report every year. We're in advertising businesses (garbled) and this year it's under the section "Help, Help." I tell them the kinds of businesses we want to buy. This fellow had seen that in Cincinnati, wrote me a letter and said, "I'm your guy." And I looked at him and said, "You are my guy." We bought out all the venture capitalists, but we kept the family in. And they run the business. It's that kind of thing that comes along.

The Scott Fetzer company, which is 20 other businesses, World Book, Kirby, 20 others, Campbell Hausfeld, almost a billion of sales. They had been a New York Stock Exchange company and there was a takeover attempt, even Ivan Boesky was involved, they had a whole raft of things. I'd never met the fellow then. I wrote him a letter, I said, "Dear Mr. Schey: Here's what we are..." I sent him an annual report and said, "If you want to do businesses with someone whose checks will clear, who won't bother you, here's all the shoes that will drop (I told him all the bad things about us), a one-page letter. Sent it. (Kind of difficult to get all the bad things about us on one page.) I said, "If you want to talk about it, I'll meet you, and if you don't, throw the letter away." He called me up. We met on a Sunday in Chicago, made a deal that night and in a week the deal was done. That was five or six years ago – I've been to Cleveland twice, not because I needed to be. He runs that business exactly like he [owned it himself]. Ninety-seven million dollars pretax earnings.

[Question from audience: Is everything in the stock market valued just right is it possible to find 'deals'?]

I don't know if everybody could hear that. In that past, at least in some departments, you've heard that there is no such thing as buying an undervalued stock, or making money in stocks, that the market is efficient, and that everything is priced right at all times relative to the known information about it. Therefore, there's no use thinking.

And, of course, from my standpoint I'd like to have everyone believe that, because it's a terrific advantage to be in a game where your opponent has been taught not to think. I wish the people I played Bridge would. An appreciable percentage of the money in Wall Street is managed by people who believe that. It's the old story that if there's a $20 bill on the floor there's no sense picking it up because it can't be there. That thinking, I would say, prevailed extensively 10 years ago. I would say there's a little less of it now. All I can tell you is it simply isn't true.

The last class I told of how, in 1966 or so, we bought 5% of the Disney Company for $4 million. The whole company was selling for $80 million! They'd written off all their films, Snow White, Three Little Pigs, Fantasia, all 220 some of them, written down to zero. You got 300 acres down in Anaheim and all of Disneyland for zero. The Pirate Ride had just been put in that year – $17 million it cost, yet the whole company was selling for $80 million. It was a joke. Mary Poppins made $30 million that year.

They were going to recycle Mary Poppins seven years later, they were going to recycle Snow White seven years later. It's like an oil field where the oil seeps back in, and every seven years a new crop of kids comes along and they all want to see Snow White. And they drive their parents crazy until they get to see it.

Well, that whole company was selling for $80 million. You don't have to be a financial analyst, you don't have to be finance major, to know that's a ridiculous valuation. Eleven million people a year go to Disneyland. That's seven bucks a person and you get the (garbled) thrown in free. It was a joke. And Walt Disney would tell you, if you went out to see him, would tell you all about the values, and what he had planned. It just happens occasionally in securities.

Now, an efficient market theorist would tell you that $80 million is the correct value on the Walt Disney Company. And he's wrong. You do not have to have very many like that in a lifetime. It's not very esoteric, it does not require some insight into what's going to cure AIDS, or what's going to be the best computer five years from now, or the best software manufacturer – it doesn't require anything like that. It just requires figuring out whether people will be eating Hershey bars or drinking Coca Cola.

This company [Coke] you could have bought one share of stock for $40 in 1919, when they went public. If you reinvested the dividends, you'd be worth a million now. There are 150 countries in the world where they sell this and in every single one of them per capital consumption goes up every year. It's not that complicated.

The Chairman of your [Notre Dame's] Board, Don Keough – I don't know if you're familiar with that; he is also the President of Coca Cola – used to live across the street from me in Omaha in 1960. He was a coffee salesman for Butternut Coffee, making $200 a week. And if you knew Don Keough there was no way that, if you put Don Keough together with Coke, you were going to miss. There really isn't any way they won't be selling a lot more Coca Cola products five years from now than they are now. And, they'll be making more money on each one. If you raise the price of each one of these a penny, it's $2 billion a year.

[Question from audience: Have LBOs and junk bonds hurt the country in some fundamental way in terms of its competitiveness vis-a-vis the world]

The question is whether LBOs and junk bonds and so on have hurt the country in some fundamental way in terms of its competitiveness vis-a-vis the world. I wouldn't go that far, but I think on balance it's been a huge minus on the financial scene. Extreme leverage has been, generally speaking, a net minus. The analogy has been made (and there's just enough truth to it to get you in trouble) that in buying some company with enormous amounts of debt, that it's somewhat like driving a car down the road and placing a dagger on the steering wheel pointed at your heart. If you do that, you will be a better driver – that I can assure you. You will drive with unusual care. You also, someday, will hit a small pothole, or a piece of ice, and you will end up gasping. You will have fewer accidents, but when they come along, they'll be fatal. Essentially, that's what some of corporate America did in the last 10 years. And it was motivated by huge fees. And it was motivated by greed.

The most extreme case I saw was a television station. About three years ago, a television station in Tampa sold for an amount where, when they had to borrow the money, the interest amounted to more than the total sales of the station. If everybody donated their labor, if they donated their programming, if they donated their utilities, they still wouldn't have enough to pay the interest. They went crazy. And you can buy those bonds at 15 cents on the dollar. Charlie Keating's enterprise [Lincoln Savings and Loan Association in California, which became the nation's largest thrift failure] had a bunch of them too. There's a lot of crazy stuff that went on in the last five or six years. The fees on that deal, they paid $365 million for the station, they borrowed $385 million and you can guess where the extra money went. It went into the pockets of the people who put the deal together.

[Question from audience: Is it comparable to say the same thing about companies and our government debt?]

No, it really isn't comparable. The important thing on government debt is how much is owed externally. If this group landed on an island someplace, we were stranded, and the only person we could do business with was another islander, and we all went to work producing rice, and we worked hard eight hours, and we had just enough rice to stay alive. If we worked out some internal system where some people worked 10 hours a day, and some other people worked six hours a day, and the people who worked six hours a day "borrowed" two hours worth of rice daily from the people who worked 10 hours a day, as an island we wouldn't be getting poorer. We might have some class that owed future rice, plus interest, to the people that had saved, but we would not be any worse off. We would consume all the rice we produced each day, it's just that some of us would have claim chits on each other.

If, on the other hand, we all decided to quit working, because people on the other island would work 16 hours a day, and they would ship over eight hours a day of rice to us, so we would just eat and mail them IOU's (we'd send over a guy in a canoe each night with the IOUs, they'd send over rice every day), we'd all just sit around, but the little IOUs we sent them drew interest, and then after 10 years they said, "We would just as soon quit producing rice the next 10 years and you guys work 16 hours a day." That won't work so well, particularly if it's a different generation that's being asked to work the 16 hours a day later on to pay back the rice from the first generation.

External debt, something our country owes the rest of the world, is a whole different question than internal debt. The national debt is largely held internally, but the game is changing as we run a trade deficit. So the trade deficit is a threat, essentially, to living as well as we live now. We are, essentially, selling off a little piece of the farm every day, as we run a trade deficit in order to finance our own consumption. We've got a very big rich farm, so we can sell a little piece of that farm for a long time without hardly noticing it. It's a lot like eating a little too much over time. You never see it in any one day. You don't all of a sudden get up, all of your buttons pop, and people say, "God, you look fat!" It just doesn't happen. What happens is you just keep doing it so pleasantly until, after a while, you've got a hell of a waistline. And that is, essentially, the situation in our trade deficit. We are giving the rest of the world claim checks on us. That has consequences over time.

In fact, we sold our building to the Japanese, but it doesn't make any difference whether it's the Japanese or anybody else. We sold our buildings at ABC two years ago for about $175 million. That was equal to one day's trade defect with Japan. They sent up a bunch of VCRs and things, and we sent them the title to 54th Street and 6th Avenue. And we use up the one thing and they've got the other.

It's got sort of a poetic justice to it. As a matter of fact, in 1626, I think, Peter Minuet handed a bunch of trinkets to the Indians and they paid him the island. And now, people are handing us the trinkets, and we're giving them the island. It happens every day. The trade deficit will be $100 billion plus, and that means we are giving out IOUs to the rest of the world that will draw interest, which are claims of future production of everybody in this room.

Now the internal debt, that's an entirely different story. That person helps, but the help is commensurate with the hurt. When it goes abroad, the equation is not the same.

[Question from audience: Do you just invest domestically or also abroad?]

The question is whether we just invest domestically or also abroad. The answer to that is, in terms of buying securities, everything we've bought, almost, has been domestic. It's not that I rule out other investments. We almost bought a pretty good sized investment in England a year or two ago, and we look at things elsewhere.

The United States is a $3 trillion equity pool, a $3 trillion pool of equity investments. If you can't make money in a $3 trillion pool, you're probably not going to make money in a $6 trillion pool.

Now, Coca Cola earns 80% of its money abroad and we hold 7% of that. Our 7% share is roughly $100 million. Of that, roughly $80 million comes from abroad. Coca Cola is spending an enormous amount of money in East Germany in the next year. They were in there big in March of 1990. Interestingly enough, the first Coca Cola they sold in East Germany, you may be too young for this, but it was shipped from Dunkirk where the Germans, essentially, drove the English into the sea 50 years ago. For a while all the Coca Cola was going from our big bottling plant in Dunkirk to East Germany. Now, the infrastructure has been built up within East Germany tremendously, and it will be a good market for Coke.

Coke is also in McDonald's in Moscow. The Moscow McDonald's is doing $235,000 in business a day, 50 times the average McDonald's in this country. You think of 50 McDonald's opening and that's how much business that Moscow McDonald's has done. That's a lot of people buying Coke.

[Question from audience: Have you changed your ideas over the years as your bank account has increased?]

The question was, "Have I changed my ideas over the years as my bank account has increased?" The truth is, I used to have more ideas than money and now I've got more money than ideas. You've put your finger on that particular problem, but there are worse problems.

The only ideas we're interested in now are big ideas. We are not interested in anything that we do not think we can put at least $100 million into, usually quite a bit more. We own fewer stocks now, with $7 or $8 billion, than we owned back when we had $15 million in 1970.

We do not try and buy more and more of everything. I call that the Noah's Ark approach to investing – have two of everything. We've got a very selective ark, and we only want a couple of specimens on there. It makes it more difficult, but you don't need very many good ideas. If we get one good idea a year, that would be terrific. And if you negotiate with me, you'd get me down to one every two or three years. That's all you need. You do not have to keep hitting home runs all the time. That's one of the nice things about this business. If you make one decision on something like that, it takes care of a lot.

I always tell classes that, in the investment world, if you had a punch card when you got when you got out of school, and there were only 20 punches on it, and when that was done, you were all done investing, you'd make more money than having one with unlimited punches. You'd make sure you used them for the right things.

The big things are not what you do; they're what you don't do. Basically, we've had very few things we've lost money on. We've had no more good ideas than other people. But we've not made big mistakes – that I learned from Ben Graham. He used to say there are two rules in investing. The first: don't lose. The second: don't forget the first.

[Question from audience: Does the current recession change your attitude toward investing? And are there any special industries you favor?]

The first question was, "Does the current recession change our attitude toward investing?" It doesn't change it a nickel's worth. If something comes along tomorrow that's interesting, I will do it tomorrow. And it will be by exactly the same yardsticks I used whenever the business cycle was at its peak. We don't care what businesses are doing. If the Chairman of the Federal Reserve called me tonight and said, "I am really panicking and things are terrible," I don't care. We will do exactly what we were going to do tomorrow morning. The truth is, on balance, we will do more business when people are pessimistic. Not because we like pessimism, but because it makes for prices that are much more attractive. If you all have filling stations to sell in South Bend, I want to do business with whoever is most negative about filling stations. And that's were I'm going to make the best buy. Times are really good and times are really bad, over a period of time.

We don't quit selling candy in July just because it isn't Christmas. We pay *no* attention to economic forecasts. I don't read anything [along those lines]. I read annual reports, but I don't read anybody's opinion about what's going to happen next week, or next month or next year.

The second question is whether there are any special industries we favor. The only thing we favor is industries we can understand. And then, we like businesses with what I call "moats" around them. We like businesses that are protected in some way from competition. If you go in the drugstore and say, "I want to buy a Hershey bar" and the guy says, "I've got an unmarked chocolate bar that's a nickel cheaper," you'll buy the Hershey bar or you'll go across the street.

One of the interesting things to do is walk through a supermarket sometime and think about who's got pricing power, and who's got a franchise, and who doesn't. If you go buy Oreo cookies, and I'm going to take home Oreo cookies or something that looks like Oreo cookies for the kids, or your spouse, or whomever, you'll buy the Oreo cookies. If the other is three cents a package cheaper, you'll still buy the Oreo cookies. You'll buy Jello instead of some other. You'll buy Kool-Aid instead of Wyler's powdered soft drink. But, if you go to buy milk, it doesn't make any difference whether it's Borden's, or Sealtest, or whatever. And you will not pay a premium to buy one milk over another. You will not pay a premium to buy one [brand of] frozen peas over another, probably. It's the difference between having a wonderful business and not a wonderful business. The milk business is not a good business.

In our candy business, Valentine's is coming up, and See's

Candy on the West Coast is a very desirable item, and very few men will want to hand their girlfriend, or wife, or whatever, and say, "Here, honey, I took the low bid." It just doesn't sell. We want things where they're not terribly price sensitive. And if you're going to go out and buy a car this afternoon, you're not going to say, "I'd like that red job there, but I want to be sure it has steel that came from Bethlehem steel." You don't care where the steel came from.

And, therefore, Bethlehem's got nothing to say to General Motors, or Ford, except what wonderful guys they are. And General Motors says, "We know you're wonderful guys, and so, if Y sells it for X dollars a ton and you'd better be $5 under them." Anything that differentiates your product – those are the businesses we like to be in.

We like to be in businesses I can understand. There are all kinds of businesses I don't understand, but we're not going to own them. Thomas Watson Sr., of IBM, in that book *Father, Son, and Company*, that his son wrote, quoted his father as saying, "I'm no genius, but I'm smart in spots, and I stay around those spots." The real trick is knowing what you know and what you don't know. It isn't how much you know, it's whether you can define it well, so you know when you can take a swing at the ball, and you know when you've got no business swinging.

[Question from audience: How do you know if a franchise will be a good business?]

The durability and strength of the franchise is the most important thing in figuring out [whether it's a good business]. If you think a business is going to be around 10 or 20 years from now, and that they're going to be able to price advantageously, that's going to be a good business. And if somebody has to have a prayer session every time they want to raise the price a dollar a pound on whatever they're selling, that's not going to be a good business.

104

What's the highest priced daily newspaper in the United States? Most of you are familiar with it. The highest priced daily newspaper in the United States, with any circulation at all, is the *Daily Racing Form*. It sells about 150,000 copies a day, and it has for about 50 years, and it's either $2.00 or $2.25 (they keep raising prices) and it's essential. If you're heading to the racetrack and you've got a choice between betting on your wife's birthday, and Joe's Little Green Sheet, and the *Daily Racing Form*, if you're a serious racing handicapper, you want *The Form*. You can charge $2.00 for *The Form*, you can charge $1.50, you can charge $2.50 and people are going to buy it. It's like selling needles to addicts, basically. It's an essential business. It will be an essential business five or 10 years from now.

You have to decide whether horse racing will be around five or 10 years from now, and you have to decide whether there's any way people will get their information about past performances of different horses from different sources. But you've only got about two questions to answer, and if you answer them, you know the business will make a lot of money. *The Form* has huge profit margins, incidentally. Wider than any other newspaper. They charge what they want to basically. It's an easy to understand business – so easy to understand.

Snow White is going to show up every so often, and when she shows up, millions of kids are going, and they'll make their money, and they don't have to make the picture again. Made back in 1937 or so. It's a perpetual royalty on youth. And that's not a bad business.

[Question from audience: Where did Donald Trump go wrong?]

Where did Donald Trump go wrong? The big problem with Donald Trump was he never went right. He basically overpaid for properties, but he got people to lend him the money. He was terrific at borrowing money. If you look at his assets, and what he paid for them, and what he borrowed to get them, there was never any real equity there.

He owes, perhaps, $3.5 billion now, and, if you had to pick a figure as to the value of the assets, it might be more like $2.5 billion. He's a billion in the hole, which is a lot better than being $100 in the hole because if you're $100 in the hole, they come and take the TV set. If you're a billion in the hole, they say, "Hang in there, Donald."

It's interesting why smart people go astray. That's one of the most interesting things in business. I've seen all sorts of people with terrific IQs that end up flopping in Wall Street or business because they beat themselves. They have 500-horsepower engines, and get 50-horsepower out of them. Or, worse than that, they have their foot on the brake and the accelerator at the same time. They really manage to screw themselves up.

I tried this with the last class. Let's say each one of you could buy 10% of the earnings, forever, of anybody else in this room, except me. Let's charge $50,000. And that means that if somebody gets out of here and earns $30,000 you get a $3,000 royalty off them. But, if they do extremely well, and become President of Coca Cola like Don Keough did, you'll make a fortune.

How are you going to think, in terms of the rest of the people here, of which one you want to buy the 10% of? Let's say we had Donald Trump here, and my friend Tom Murphy, who runs ABC, or Don Keough, and you're really betting on the lifetime of each of them, and let's say they're all in equally good health. Would you give them an IQ test? Well, you'd want to be certain they have a certain amount of IQ.

Would you want to measure how strongly motivated they were, how much they wanted to get rich? Donald Trump wanted to get rich. That might not be a great qualifier. What would you do to select that one person out of this whole crowd here, because there will be a huge difference in results here.

There's not a huge difference in IQ. But there will be a huge difference in results. I would venture to say, I don't know how well this group knows each other, you come from two different schools, so I'd break it down into two groups, I would venture to say that your guesses would not be bad. They'd be better if you'd had more experience with the group, and if you've had more experience generally, but they will be way better than flipping coins.

You would probably relate it to a lot of qualities, some of which would be straight from Ben Franklin – I would suggest that the big successes I've met had a fair amount of Ben Franklin in them. And Donald Trump did not.

One of the things you will find, which is interesting and people don't think of it enough, with most businesses and with most individuals, life tends to snap you at your weakest link. So it isn't the strongest link you're looking for among the individuals in the room. It isn't even the average strength of the chain. It's the weakest link that causes the problem. It may be alcohol, it may be gambling, it may be a lot of things, it may be nothing, which is terrific. But it is a real weakest link problem.

When I look at our managers, I'm not trying to look at the guy who wakes up at night and says, "E = MC 2," or something. I am looking for people that function very, very well. And that means not having any weak links. The two biggest weak links in my experience: I've seen more people fail because of liquor and leverage – leverage being borrowed money. Donald Trump failed because of leverage. He simply got infatuated with how much money he could borrow, and he did not give enough thought to how much money he could pay back.

You really don't need leverage in this world much. If you're smart, you're going to make a lot of money without borrowing. I've never borrowed a significant amount of money in my life. Never. Never will. I've got no interest in it. The other reason is I never thought I would be way happier when I had 2X instead of

X. You ought to have a good time all the time as you go along. If you say, "I'm taking this job – I don't really like this job but in three years it will lead to this," forget it. Find one you like right now.

Warren Buffett Answers Tough College Questions

Follow Warren Buffett's 1994 intriguing Q&A session with America's finest up & coming businessmen, as he addresses The University of Nebraska-Lincoln College of Business Administration. Encouraging the audience to ask questions "as tough and impertinent as you like because it makes it more interesting for me," Mr. Buffett fields questions on a wide array of topics, from business to sports to personal to political. This is one lecture you don't want to miss!

Lecture of The E. J. Faulkner Lecture Series

A Colloquium with University of Nebraska-Lincoln Students
By Warren E. Buffett
Chairman of the Board Berkshire Hathaway, Inc.
Sponsored by Woodmen Accident and Life Company, in conjunction with The College of Business Administration-Lincoln
October 10, 1994

WARREN E. BUFFETT

Warren E. Buffett is Chairman of the Board and Chief Executive Officer of Berkshire Hathaway Inc., a company controlled by Buffett Partnerships, Ltd. from 1965. Berkshire Hathaway Inc.'s business activities include underwriting of property and casualty insurance, candy production and sales at retail, newspaper publishing, retailing home furnishings, sales of encyclopedias, sales of home cleaning units, manufacture and distribution of uniforms, retail jewelry, and manufacture, import, and distribution of furniture.

Mr. Buffett is perhaps the most highly regarded businessperson in the United States today. His advice is widely sought, and highly treasured. He serves as a Director of Capital City/ABC, the Coca-Cola Company, the Gillette Company, Salomon Inc. and USAir Group, Inc. Berkshire Hathaway has significant investments in each of these companies. His investment acumen, buttressed by the force of his reputation, honesty, and integrity were instrumental in the preservation of one of the oldest and largest investment banking houses in the world, Salomon Brothers.

Berkshire Hathaway's annual report, authored by Mr. Buffett, is widely read in the business and investment community for its sound advice, its creativity, and its humor in explaining important principles for achieving success in business. The Berkshire annual meeting has become an "event," which not only spreads the Buffett message but enhances Berkshire's corporate coffers through visitations by shareholders to Omaha's Nebraska Furniture Mart and Borsheim's Jewelry Store, both of which are in the Berkshire Hathaway stable.

Mr. Buffett was born in Omaha to Howard H. Buffett and Leila Stahl Buffett. His father, an investment banker, served as congressman from Nebraska's second district from 1943-1949 and from 1951-1953. Mr. Buffett married Susan Thompson in April 1952. They have three children - Susan, Howard, and Peter.

Mr. Buffett graduated from Woodrow Wilson High School in Washington, D.C. in 1947, attended the Wharton School of Finance at the University of Pennsylvania from 1947-1949 and received a Bachelor of Science degree in Business Administration from the University of Nebraska in 1950. In 1951 he received a Masters degree in Economics from Columbia University. His mentor, Benjamin Graham, was one of his professors at Columbia. Mr. Buffett serves as Life Trustee of Grinnell College; Life Trustee of the Urban Institute; Trustee of the Business Enterprise Trust, Stanford, California; Trustee of the Wellness Council of the Midlands; and as a member of the American Academy of Arts and Science. His foundation is reported to provide funding mainly on world population issues and nuclear disarmament.

Mr. Buffett resides in Omaha, Nebraska and presides over his financial empire from that city without the "luxury" of a large staff, computer modeling or Wall Street gossip.

The University of Nebraska-Lincoln College of Business Administration and Woodmen Accident and Life Company take great pleasure in welcoming Warren E. Buffett as the 1994 E. J. Faulkner lecturer.

E. J. Faulkner Lecture
October 10, 1994
Warren E. Buffett

Introduction of Warren Buffett by Mr. John Haessler

President and Chief Executive Officer Woodmen Accident and Life Company

It's a great pleasure for me, both personally and on behalf of Woodmen, to welcome you to this lecture, which is 16th in a series that Woodmen has sponsored in conjunction with the College of Business Administration. We have established this lecture, as I think many of you know, in honor of E. J. Faulkner, who served for 60 years with Woodmen, 44 years as a CEO. He was a great friend and a graduate of the campus and of the College of Business Administration. Through his estate, a gift has been made and it is now being translated into the writing lab at the College of Business Administration.

We are greatly privileged and especially pleased to have Warren Buffett here. From the size of this crowd and excitement, the anticipation that's been on campus is obviously honored in the halls of the academia as well as in business. While he needs no introduction, I think he truly deserves one. And frankly, he deserves one that will be more laudatory and flattering than I will

111

give him, because I don't think a flowery one would comport with his sense of comfort. He's a very basic man.

Much of the activity of Mr. Buffett is highlighted on the handout that you received. He is a native Nebraskan. He was born in Omaha. He went to high school in Washington, D.C. His father, who was an investment banker, also served as a congressman from the second district - Republican by the way. (Warren Buffett and I are probably the only two Democrats in this whole room.)

He received his degree from the University of Nebraska College of Business Administration; he then went to Columbia University for a Masters, where he studied under Benjamin Graham, who was a friend and mentor for his life. He started, as I think many of you know, modestly in the mid-50s with a limited partnership, some friends and some relatives and about $100,000 of his money. He's built that into the financial empire of Berkshire Hathaway, and he has now become the richest person in America.

Now, I know that some of you have seen *Forbes,* and Bill Gates has supposedly passed him in the last year. But nobody wants to tell Warren that. Today, we're going to say he is the richest person in the United States. Besides, we'd already invited him before he slipped.

But wealth is not a very good definer of the man. He has said he enjoys the process far more than the proceeds, and I think that's true. He got his wealth the old fashioned way - he earned it. And he did it not by the sweat of his brow, but by leveraging his brain. And he did it by using his own assets and not somebody else's, and certainly not somebody else's debt. He did it by thinking, and that doesn't sound too unique but in one of his annual reports, he quotes the observation of Burton Russell, "that most men would rather die than think and many do." And he says this applies with unusual force in the financial world. Not only is he a thinker, he's an investor; he's not a speculator; he builds; he doesn't tear down. He creates jobs; he doesn't displace persons. And talking about investing and speculation, he writes, "Indeed, we believe that according the name 'investors' to institutions that trade actively is like calling someone who repeatedly engages in one-night stands a romantic.'"

In his annual reports that you've read avidly, he quotes unusual people. Talking about diversity as not being necessarily good, he quotes Mae West, "Too much of a good thing can be wonderful." In talking about extracting himself from a bad deal that he felt was a bargain when he went into it, he refers to a gentleman in a country western song that said, "My wife ran away with my best friend and I still miss him a lot." His style, his humility, his lack of pretense is probably best represented or at least well represented in setting up some details for this lecture. One of the questions was, "Do you want extra security here?" His answer, "We don't need any security, just ask the attendees to check any soft fruit at the door."

Ladies and Gentlemen, it is a great pleasure to present a true legend in his own time, the oracle of Omaha, Warren E. Buffett.

WARREN BUFFET'S OPENING REMARKS AND CONVERSATION WITH STUDENTS:

Testing. One million, two million, three million... Somebody yelled out from the back earlier, "I can't hear you." I was giving a speech a few weeks ago and the same thing happened. Somebody said, "I can't hear you." And, then someone in the front stood up and said, "I can - let's change places."

It's really good to be here today. I have a lot of great memories of the University. My mother and father met here when my dad was editor of the *Daily Nebraskan* in 1924. My mother had worked for her father's tiny paper in West Point. And so, when she came here, she went into the *Daily Nebraskan* to apply for a job and met my dad there.

Within a couple of years, they were married. Then about twenty-five years later or thereabouts, after two years at the Wharton School at the University of Pennsylvania, I transferred here and I must say that I thought that my year here was considerably superior to either of the years I'd had at Wharton.

I got a lot of education. Ray Dein from here was a terrific accounting professor at that time. We were reminiscing earlier a little bit about Carl Arndt, who taught Economics. Professor Arndt, when he taught Economics, would leave the room during the exams. We thought that was very trusting of him. He explained that, well, he could do that because, although we had the same exam, he had different answers for the odd and even numbered seats.

I would like to talk to the students, primarily, a little bit about your future because an experience I had a couple of years ago may tie in with that. Then we'll get into questions and what's on your mind. But I did have an experience in 1991 that may have some applicability to you students in the room.

What happened then was that on a Friday, August 14, 1991, I received a phone call at a quarter of seven in the morning. And, it woke me up, I'm sorry to admit. That early-to-bed, early-to-rise stuff is, well, you can forget that. I'm not going to give you any of that. In any event, I got this call and on the other end were some people in a conference room, obviously on a speakerphone. They told me that the top management of Salomon had been told the previous night, by the President of the New York Federal Reserve Bank (and he is the most important man in financial markets in the world; he is not that well known, the Chairman of the Fed would be better known), but the President of the New York Fed, in terms of financial markets is number one, and his name is Jerry Congan. Mr. Congan had told the top management of Salomon that they were unacceptable to be running the institution, and he meant, immediately. So they decided the next morning that they were going to leave. They had to leave. And they were calling to say that as of that time there was no one there to run the institution.

That was a rather serious situation because at that time, Salomon owed more money than any other institution in the United States, with the exception of Citicorp, the big bank. Citicorp owed a little over $200 billion. Salomon's total liabilities were just under $150 billion.

Now, $150 billion was roughly equal to the profits of all of the companies on the New York Stock Exchange in that year. So, it was more money than the Bank of America owed. It was more money than American Express owed. It was more money than Fannie Mae owed.

Only Citicorp owed more money. The problem about this $150 billion was that basically, it almost all came due within the next couple of weeks. Unlike Citicorp or the Bank of America or Manny Hanny or the other big banks, people who had lent money to Salomon were not protected by FDIC insurance, so they could not look to the government that way. And, they were also not protected by what's called the "Too Big To Fail Doctrine".

Basically, people feel, although the Fed has not been terribly specific about it, that any of the really big banks will not be allowed to fail because the Fed is worried about a domino effect. So, if people were worried about the solvency of Citicorp or Chase or somebody like that, they didn't really worry about their deposits there because they had both FDIC insurance and they had this "Too Big To Fail Doctrine". Salomon had neither.

So we were faced with the fact that all over the world, because this money was owed all over the world, that people on that Friday and the following Monday were going to want us to pay back $140 odd billion or something close to it, which is not the easiest thing to do.

I went to New York that afternoon, and I met with Mr. Corigan that night. I won't forget that because when I went in, in kind of a light way, I said to Mr. Corigan, "The only thing I owe personally is $70,000 on a second home I have in California and that is because the interest rate is cheap. I may need a little help," and I smiled kind of weakly. He gave me this steely look and he said, "Prepare for all eventualities".

I didn't know exactly what he meant by that but I certainly thought of strychnine or something of the sort. So anyway, one immediate problem I had was that my basic job was going to be dealing with regulators and Congress and all that sort of thing. And, essentially, we had to reassure the world, between that Friday night and the following Monday morning, that Salomon was not going to collapse or we were going to have a run on the bank.

This is where the story starts becoming applicable to this group. One of the things I immediately had to do was to find somebody to run the place. This was a company with 8,000 employees, perhaps 500 or more in Tokyo and 1,000 or more in London. And, spread all over the world, we owed $10 or $15 billion in Japan and similar amounts in Europe. So, there was a real problem in terms of who was actually going to run the place day to day.

This is a company that, because it has a very big government securities operation, now does over $200 billion of business a day. You don't make very much money on it, but that's close to three times as much business as Wal-Mart does in a year. Now, it is a different sort of business, but it does require someone who knows what is going on, and I didn't know the business or the details of the business at all. So, I was faced on that Friday night with the problem of deciding who would run this place and then making a recommendation to the Board, that was going to meet on Sunday.

There were about a dozen candidates for that job who were high up in Salomon. I only knew four or five of them by their faces. I knew most of the twelve by name, but I only had met four or five of them. This was the most important hiring decision in my life.

I hope all of you are going to go out and get hired in the next few years. And, it might be interesting to know what went through my mind in making that important hiring decision because it may be going through the minds of some of the people that you will be facing in the next few years. What I did was interview those twelve people. We had one discussion on Friday night because they were in an uproar about something or other, and then the next morning, I interviewed these people serially over a three- or four-hour period.

Now, the good news is that I did not ask them their grades in business school. You can relax. But the bad news is, of course, that I didn't even ask them whether they went to business school. I did not ask for their resume.

I never saw a resume on the fellow that I decided on. I really had to decide in that time who was going to be the best person for me to go into a fox hole with and who was going to be able to lead this organization during an extremely difficult period, when people would be quitting, when customers would be badgering them, and when lenders would be pulling out - all of that sort of thing. I didn't give them an IQ test. I had twelve people there who all were smart enough to run the place. And, most of the people in this room, a very significant majority, would be smart enough to run the place.

Most businesses do not require somebody with a staggering IQ. I wasn't looking for Forrest Gump, either. But, the dozen or so had all the IQ necessary; they had all the drive necessary. These are people who were used to working twelve-hour days and had lots of push. So, it was not a question of energy. It was a question of who, in my view, with both of those qualities already a given, really was the highest quality individual.

It was the person who would not stick a gun to my head after he took the job, because I couldn't afford to fire whoever came in and I couldn't afford to have him quit on me when the going got tough a week or two weeks or month later, because with one more event like that, it would have been curtains. So, I really had to be sure of the steadfastness of the individual. I had to be sure he was up to it temperamentally, because the pressures would be enormous.

The person I decided on never asked me then; he never asked me a week later; he never asked me a month later, what the pay was. Basically, he was a battlefield promotion and he behaved like he was a battlefield promotion. He could have come to me and said, "Look, I could go over to Goldman Sachs and make 'X' this year and this is going to be much tougher so I want 150% of 'X' from you".

He never said a word about that. As a matter a fact, in the first year, just to set an example, he reduced his pay, running the whole place for less than he had made running the Tokyo office the year before. He never asked me to indemnify him against the lawsuits that would be forthcoming if the place failed. If things had gone bad, and you couldn't tell whether they would or not, we were going to get sued by everybody in the world. And, if Salomon had gone under, its indemnification would have been no good. So, it would have been perfectly reasonable for this person to say, "Well, look, I'll take this job but who knows what's going to happen and if it happens, Salomon isn't going to be good for it.

So why doesn't Berkshire Hathaway or why don't you personally indemnify me against the lawsuits I'll be facing the rest of my life if this goes sour?" He never said a word about it. It wasn't because he was dumb and didn't know enough to ask that. He just felt it was not the right thing to do under those circumstances. So, in the end, I picked out the individual there who I felt was an outstanding human being. He never let me down.

He took on that job the next day. We came out of a directors' meeting at three in the afternoon. And there were these twelve people out there and I just walked up to him and said to him, "You're it, pal". And, we went right from there down the elevator to meet a couple hundred reporters who had come in on a Sunday afternoon and who were plenty hostile in some ways. He sat up there on the stage with me and answered questions for three hours. And I knew then I had made the right choice.

Now, the interesting thing about that choice is that the qualities that attracted me to him were not impossible for anyone to achieve. He didn't have to be able to jump seven feet. He didn't have to be able to throw a football sixty yards. He didn't have to be able to remember every bridge hand he played the previous year or something of the sort. There was no feat of intellect or something like that. What he did was bring qualities like steadfastness and honesty. I knew he would tell me the bad news. I always worry about that with people who work for me. They don't need to tell me the good news. I just want to hear the bad news.

I knew he would not get his ego involved in decisions. I knew he would not be envious or greedy or all of those things that make people unattractive. And, the truth is, that anybody can have those same qualities that Deryck Maughan, the fellow I picked, exhibited. They are not feats that are beyond anyone. They are simply a matter of deciding what you are going to do and what kind of person you are going to make out of yourself, and then doing it.

John mentioned Ben Graham, who was my teacher at Columbia University. When he was twelve years old, he sat down and made a list of the qualities he admired in other people; and he made a list also of the qualities that he found unattractive in other people. He decided that it was just an act of will and then habit to develop those attractive qualities and to get rid of the unattractive qualities.

Anybody can show up on time; they cannot claim credit for ideas that are not their own; they cannot cut corners; they can avoid envy. All of those things are doable and they make an enormous difference in how you function, not only in your job, but in society, subsequently.

I'll give one more illustration. Let's just assume when you got out of school, that you won a lottery of some sort and you were entitled to pick one of your classmates, and you got 10% of the earnings of that classmate for the rest of his or her life. You had about an hour to make up your mind. Now we'll leave out picking the son or daughter of the richest person around or something of the sort. Let's say we're all starting from scratch. Now, who would you pick? Just think about that for a moment.

You wouldn't give them an IQ test. You probably wouldn't look at their grades. You'd probably think, who's going to function best when they get out there? If they had a 300 horsepower motor, who's going to get 300 horsepower out of it instead of 150 or 100? You'd look for who is going to function best. And, you would look for people with those qualities that you admire, but which are also attainable by you and which become a matter of habit after time.

Somebody said that the chains of habit are too light to be felt until they're too heavy to be broken. It's absolutely true that the habits of behavior you start out with will follow you the rest of your life. And, as you think about that person whom you would like to buy the 10% of, the person whom you find admirable or attractive, the answer is that if you want to sit down and do it yourself, you can be the one that you would buy 10% of.

It is not that difficult. One friend of mine said that in hiring they look for three things: intelligence, energy, and character. If they don't have the last one, the first two will kill you because, it's true, if you are going to hire somebody that doesn't have character, you had really better hope they are dumb and lazy, because, if they are smart and energetic, they'll get you in all kinds of trouble. Well, that's enough of the advice.

Let's tackle the questions that you are interested in. Make them as tough and impertinent as you like because it makes it more interesting for me and it probably makes it more interesting for the audience. So, feel free to throw your hard one.

QUESTIONS AND ANSWERS

E. J. Faulkner Lecture
Warren R. Buffett

Q. In a sentence or less, could you please tell me what is your personal philosophy of life? And then my follow-up question, why?

A. Well, I'm not sure I have any brilliant philosophy of life. I certainly enjoy life. I like my life as much as anybody possibly could. I mean, I love every day and one reason I do is that I am fortunate in that I only work with people I like. I consider myself very lucky to be in that position. If you work in a job where your stomach churns and you find yourself dreading going to work and all that sort of thing, essentially, that is really like marrying for money, which is probably a dumb idea under any circumstances. And, it's absolute madness if you are already rich. I've been very fortunate in that I have no stress whatsoever.

I'm going to try and outlive Mrs. B. I mean it. I tap dance on the way to work. I do believe in working at something you enjoy. I gave this advice one time at Harvard when somebody asked me, "Who should I work for?" I said, "Well, go work for somebody you admire. You're bound to get a good result." A couple of weeks later, I received a call from the Dean, and he said, "What did you tell that group? They've all decided to become self-employed!"

Q. If you could look in your crystal ball, what kind of sector stocks would you look into in the next few years? What kind of stocks do you think will boom?

A. That's an academic question, if I ever heard one. Just a little theoretical.

Q. What exactly do you do all day?

A. Getting right to the core here, aren't you? I spend an inordinate amount of time reading. I probably read at least six hours a day, maybe more. And I spend an hour or two on the telephone. And I think. That's about it. We have no meetings at Berkshire. We've never had. We have businesses around the country; we have some 20,000 employees, but we've only had one meeting of our managers in the twenty-some years I've been there, to talk about health care - one time. But, they never come to Omaha.

We never have presentations. We don't have a slide projector. We don't do any of that sort of thing. Our board of directors meets once a year, right after the annual meeting. We have lunch and that's it, because I hate meetings, frankly. I have created something that I enjoy. I happen to enjoy reading a lot, and I happen to enjoy thinking about things. It is a little crazy, it seems to me, if you are building a business and creating a business, not to create something you are going to enjoy when you get through. It's like painting a painting. I mean, you ought to paint something you are going to enjoy looking at when you get through.

Now, I know I'm avoiding your first question about what I should buy this afternoon. I don't think much about that. I don't think at all about what the stock market will do or what given stocks will do in the very short term. We do try to own, and to look at stocks, as pieces of businesses. And, that is crucial in my view to the investing process; that is, to not think about a stock as a little ticker symbol or something that goes up or down, or something of the sort, but to think about the business that you own... Same way if you were deciding on a business to buy in Lincoln. You might think about buying a dry cleaning store or a grocery store or whatever. You wouldn't think about what this business is going to be selling for tomorrow or next week or anything. You would think about whether it's going be a good business over a long period of time. And that's what we try and do. So, if you look at the portfolio of Berkshire, you will see the kind of businesses that we like to own.

Our biggest single holding is Coca-Cola. We own a lot of Gillette. Those are two of the most dominant companies in the world in their field. And they are also companies that are not subject to a lot of change.

We don't want to own things where the world is going to change rapidly because I don't think I can see change that well or any better than the next fellow. So, I really want something that I think is going to be quite stable, that has very good economics going for it. Coca-Cola sells 47% of all the soft drinks in the world. That is seven hundred and fifty million eight-ounce servings a day around the world. That means if you increase the price of Coke one penny you would add two and a half billion dollars pre-tax to the earnings. So, that's the kind of thing I can figure out. And, Gillette, I mean Gillette is marvelous. Gillette supplies over 60% of the dollar value of razor blades in the world. When I go to bed at night and I think of all those billions of males sitting there with hair growing on their faces while I sleep, that can put you to sleep very comfortably.

Q. Have you ever thought of opening your own stock school?

A. No, I've got my occupation for the rest of my life. I plan to keep running Berkshire Hathaway.

Q. The problem with money is that it tends to flow toward the emotional part of the human being. And, I guess what fascinates me about you, in what I have observed in the media and so forth, is that you tend to keep a clear, cool head. For example, when you hired that fellow from the Tokyo office, you were adding up certain factors that were tangibles. I wonder if you do the same when you buy stocks, and what happens when they turn out to be "dogs", like USAir and Salomon Brothers. Obviously, those didn't pan out as expected when you bought them; however in the fullness of time, one can never tell.

A. You can probably tell on one of them, anyway.

Q. If you are talking about Salomon Brothers, I think you once referred to them as a cash cow; however, when you buy a stock like that, how much of it is just simply a result of Warren Buffett's many, many years of reading six hours, making phone calls, and thinking at night? Or, how much of it comes down to a gambler's feel or intuition? Is it that much?

A. I would say there is no hunch or intuitiveness or anything of the sort. I mean, I try to sit down and figure out what the future economic prospects of a business are. I try to figure out whether the management is someone or some group I both trust and admire, and I try to figure out whether the price is right. I mean that: It's the right business, the right people, and the right price. There are a whole bunch of businesses I don't know the answer on. If you take all the companies on the New York Stock Exchange, a couple thousand plus, I don't have a view on a great many of them. I am familiar with them but I just don't have the faintest idea what is going to happen in the future. So, I try to narrow it down to what I call my "circle of competence". The important thing in your circle of competence is not how big the circle is. It isn't the area of it. It's how well you define the perimeter. So you know when you are in it, and you know when you are outside of it. And, if I have any advantage, it's probably that I know when I know what I'm doing, and I know when I don't know what I'm doing. That's key in the securities business. You have to make very few correct decisions in securities to get very rich. You don't have to do a hundred smart things. If we do one smart thing a year, (a) my partner will be surprised, and (b) that's plenty. I mean, that's more than enough. And, that's all I want to do. So, I'm looking for the one idea.

But you are correct that everything I look at over the years, all the reading I do and everything, comes together at some point in terms of giving me the feeling that this particular decision is within my "circle of competence". And, when it is within it, I'm willing to go *very* big. I do not believe in taking baby steps when you see something that you really understand. I never want to do anything on a small scale because, what's the reason? If I'm doing it on a small scale because I'm not that sure of my opinion, I'll forget it entirely and go onto something I'm sure about.

Q. Yesterday in the *World Herald,* it was reported that a multi-millionaire with no blood relatives left $5.6 million to the U.S. government.
A. I saw that.

Q. And that money would cover less than two minutes of government spending. If you had no blood relatives and no charitable foundation, would you leave your money to the government? Assuming, of course, it would take longer to spend your fortune.
A. Well, I have one of the blood relatives here today who's monitoring what I'm saying. I read the other day about a fellow who left all of his money to his wife on the condition that she would remarry, so at least one man would mourn his passing. I would say this, when you rule out the philanthropic, that gets tough. If you leave it to the government, you're leaving it to society, basically. I would rather leave it to people, very high-grade intelligent people, to spend in the interests of society rather than simply to reduce the debt or the deficit that year. You know, if you told me that I couldn't leave it to an individual or to charity, I mean, at that point 1 would be pretty much stuck. It would be like having a 100% estate tax, in effect.

I would say that I got my money from society. If you stuck me down in the middle of Bangladesh or Peru, I wouldn't be worth a damn. I have some talents that are particularly suited to this particular economy. I get a lot from society. I get to live exactly the kind of life I want to live; and then not to give it back to society seems a little crazy to me. So, essentially, everything I have will go back. And, I will not try to direct what the trustees do ahead of time. I just want to pick very high-grade people, smart people, very few people because if you get a large group, it will bureaucratize. I've got six trustees on the foundation and they will do a much better job above ground after I die than will be done if I start giving them instructions from beneath the ground. I'm very satisfied with the arrangement. The only thing I've instructed them to do is try and do something big. I don't believe in lots of little things.

Q. Well, we certainly hope you live to be 150, 200. Someone with your character needs to stay around.
A. Thank you. Thank you.

Q. I was wondering if you had a role model.
A. Yes. I call them heroes, but I've had a half a dozen or so heroes in my live. I've been extremely fortunate in that none of my heroes ever let me down. I never, never had a situation where I was disappointed in any one of the half a dozen or so, starting number one with my dad. And, that's a great thing. I think it's very important to have the right heroes. Now they call them role models or whatever; but you're going to take your cues from somebody. You're going to pick up the habits, and qualities, like I talked about earlier, from somebody. Fortunately I had some terrific people who were helpful to me in that regard. I went through a period, when we first moved to Washington, where I was antisocial for a while. And, really having the right heroes pulled me through that as well as anything. So I say, choose your heroes carefully, and then figure out what it is about them that you admire. Then figure out how to do the same thing. It's not impossible.

Q. Was your investment with the Equity Fund of Nebraska a one-time offering?

A. No. About a year or so ago, the Governor, or a group connected with the Governor, organized a fund to sponsor low-income, affordable housing in the State. These funds have existed around the country and we had participated in those national funds; so he asked if we would participate in the Nebraska fund. We said yes, and we will participate in the future. I hope that the participation becomes broad, because it not only has a good social

purpose, but it's a perfectly intelligent investment. So, it is not like there is any sacrifice on our part in doing this. This is something that makes economic sense for Berkshire Hathaway. And, I would hope that other businesses around the State would join in. It's not a one-time thing.

Q. How would a young entrepreneur, like myself, get start-up cash for my business?

A. Get start-up capital? Well, that's a tough question because compound interest is a little bit like rolling a snowball down a hill. You can start with a small snowball and if it rolls down a long enough hill (and my hill's now 53 years long - that's when I bought my first stock), and the snow is mildly sticky, you'll have a real snowball at the end. And then, somebody says, "How do you get the small snowball at the top of the hill?" I don't know any way to do it except spending less than you earn and saving some money, unless you are lucky enough to inherit some.

In my own case, you know that I was always interested in investing, so I started saving when I was about six and by the time I got out of school, I had about $10,000. It is much easier to save money, obviously, before you have a family than after you have a family. I've always felt that one way to do it, if you've got a job and it's meeting your needs (in my own case, I delivered papers and that's an ideal job for a couple hours a day), is to take a second job and save all the money from that. Getting the initial stake, being ahead of the game, is enormously important in life.

It is so much better to be working from a position of strength and have a loaded gun. That may be a fairly small amount of money. Ten thousand dollars doesn't sound so big, although it was probably the equivalent of close to $100,000 now. That was my edge. If I hadn't had that, I wouldn't have had anything to work with subsequently. There isn't really any way to get capital except to spend less than you earn. That's easier when you are very young than at any other time - certainly before you have a family.

Q. Mr. Buffett, I'd just like to know if there is there is any truth to the rumor that you have been taking Cornhusker quarterback recruits out to dinner?

A. Nope. If I knew any good ones, I think I would, but... If anybody here is healthy and feels like they can throw that ball sixty yards, stand up. I've got an intense interest. I think we have the best football coach in the United States. He and Nancy are both truly outstanding human beings. I know that personally. I would love to see everything come together. I think he has had a lot of bad luck this year.

Q. Mr. Buffett, I believe the Nation's tax code does not provide the incentives for businesses and individuals to save and invest. Without these incentives, the growth of the Nation's economy is limited. Would you support a broad-based consumption tax, such as a value-added tax, combined with offsetting reductions in the capital gains tax and corporate and individual tax rates, to encourage more savings and investment in our economy?

A. Well, I would say this, for various reasons, one of which is encouraging savings, but for other reasons I would favor a progressive consumption tax - a tax where the rates go up as you consume more. I would not favor a flat tax because that's proportional. That would be like having the same tax on everybody, paying the same percentage. And, I really feel, in terms of equity, that a progressive consumption tax is the most equitable tax. I also think it would have the greatest long-term benefits, although in the short term it would actually hurt the economy. But, over time, I think it would provide more investment and that will provide essentially a higher standard of living. Unless it is progressive though, it's unfair to have that or a national sales tax or anything that's strictly proportional, because it gets very regressive and, frankly, I think those people who consume far more than their fellow man are making withdrawals from society's bank effectively when they consume. I think they should pay higher rates as they get up in the high rates of consumption.

But, I've urged a progressive consumption tax and it's achieved somewhat more currency with economists and politicians now than it had 10 or 20 years ago. It was limited to a few academic areas a couple of decades ago. Senators Nunn and Domenici put out a report about 18 months ago, where they recommended something which was equivalent to that. I think they call it USA Unlimited Savings Account. I would say this, though: The tax rates are more conducive to savings now than they were when I was down here five or six years ago. It's not like the situation has gotten worse, in terms of savings. This will sound a little Pollyanna-ish, but it is still relatively easy to save money in this country compared to most economies in the world. A consumption tax or an unlimited IRA, in effect, would make it easier. But, this is not a tough economy compared to most of those around the world in which to save.

Q. Mr. Buffett, I was just wondering if Charlie authorized the flight over today or did you have to drive?

A. This gentleman is referring to the fact that I have a partner named Charlie Munger, whose grandfather was a Federal Judge in Lincoln. Charlie actually worked in my grandfather's store, but not at the same time I did. I met him later in life and he has become my partner.

Charlie and I have been partners in business one way or another for decades. We've never had an argument. We have different opinions on things, but we get along extremely well. Charlie overdosed on Ben Franklin early in his life, so he thinks that a penny spent is a penny lost, or something like that. This is the guy who, you know, has a prayer session before he takes the bus and, therefore, when I bought a plane, I was going to put his name - "The Charles T. Munger" - on the plane just to stick it in him a little bit. Instead, I just decided to call the plane "The Indefensible!" And that is sort of like the wolf, you know, baring his throat when he is losing to another wolf! So, I did not fly here today.

But it is true that I contemplate flying to the drug store every night! I'm in love with this plane, and I'm the same person who gave all these speeches against planes in earlier years. Then I had this counter-revelation, as they call it, and now I've fallen in love with the plane and it's going to be buried with me!

Q. Mr. Buffett, does it bother you not being the richest man in America?

A. Well, as *Forbes* pointed out, they must have counted Bill Gates' house. I mean, he's got me in that department He's a good friend of mine, incidentally. We have a lot of fun together. Bill came into Borsheim's - I can tell this because he tells it - to buy an engagement ring for Melinda, his wife. He came into Borsheim's a year ago Easter. They were in Palm Springs, and he told Melinda it was time to go back to Seattle, and when they went to the plane, the pilot reported the weather in Seattle, and everything else, so it sounded as if they were going to Seattle. Then Bill kept her occupied, so she didn't notice where the sun was. They landed in Omaha on Easter Sunday about four or five o'clock. We opened Borsheim's just for them. I said to Bill on his way out, "It's none of my business - who am I to give you advice?- but when I bought an engagement ring for my wife in 1951, I spent 6% of my net worth on it!" We didn't have quite as big a day that Sunday as I'd hoped.

But as to not being the richest, the money is a by-product of something I enjoy. It's like somebody that enjoys painting; and if you can sell your paintings for a lot of money when you get through, great! If you enjoy the painting when you get through, great too! I've had as much fun working with small sums as large sums, but I have as much fun working with large sums as small sums, I might add. The same thing is true with Bill Gates. I mean, he loves what he does.

He would do it if they gave him sharks' teeth instead of cash at the end of the day. And my guess is, that helps him do it well and helps me do it well, too. But I'm keeping an eye on him. I had a dartboard that somebody gave me to select stocks. I threw darts at it but it didn't work very well. So, I sent it to him last week.

Q. Mr. Buffett, I've been led to believe that you have some musical ability. And, I want to know, do you still play the ukulele?

A. I play it very occasionally. A year from now, Mrs. B is going to attend, close to her 102nd birthday, the opening of the Rose Blumkin Performing Arts Center in Omaha, which was formerly the Astro movie theater. She bought that theater about 15 years ago, when it was going to be torn down. The reason she bought that theater is that it's the site of one of the first good things that happened to her in this country. Back in the mid-1920s, her daughter, Frances, won a prize there, a five-dollar gold piece for singing "Am I Blue?" And, at the opening a year from now, Frances is going to sing "Am I Blue?" I'll accompany her on the ukc.

About my playing the ukulele - I did play it at the Press Club with the Governor. But my next appearance will be at the Astro next fall.

Q. The quality that I value most in any leader is integrity, whether that leader be in business or a leader in government or whatever. Do you feel that leaders in business today and the government do have a high degree of integrity? And, has it declined since you started your business?

A. It's very hard to say. I think the American public thinks it's probably declined as evidenced by polls. My own feeling from a fair amount of exposure to people in a lot of arenas, including political and business, is that the pattern is not terribly different from what you would find in the population.

If you take any large group, you will have some kind of bell-shaped curve where you will find a lot of people in the middle, who, under most conditions, will behave well, but when they are in really difficult situations, they won't. You will find people who are just outstanding on the right-hand side of the curve and those are the people who are my heroes, frankly. I don't think it has changed much over the years; that's my impression. I think that's true in politics, too.

A lot of people yearn for the good old days and all that sort of thing, but I don't think the human animal changes too much. I think the only way humans change is if they get into a new culture and adopt the mores of that culture. I think it's easier to drop down, unfortunately, if you get into a kind of jungle-type culture, than to move up if you are in some monastic-type culture. But, I don't think that the culture is materially different from what I saw in politics or in business 30 years ago. There are some outstanding people in both, and they're really the ones to focus on and try to emulate.

Q. What do you think the government is currently doing that they should stop doing? And, if you were President, what would be the first change you would make?

A. If I were President, the first thing I'd do is demand a recount. That is a job I would not like to have. There are a lot of jobs I would not like to have, but that would probably be tops on the list. I think it's very tough because I've seen a little of it, and I've even experienced a little tiny bit. It's very tough to manage any extremely large organization.

Maybe Dr. Spanier will agree with me on that, too. You have a really complex organization with loads of people that have to be decision makers under you and huge budgets. That is very difficult to manage. Then think about the fact that the most time you are going to have to do the job in is eight years. Changing cultures is really tough. I've had a little experience with that. The trick in business is to get in with a culture that's already the right kind. And, we've had good luck doing that. When we invest in a Dexter Shoe or See's Candy, that is very easy, because they have grown in a certain way because the head people think about doing the right things. I think it would be very tough in government.

If I had my way, there would be a progressive consumption tax. There wouldn't necessarily be a balanced budget. But, the national debt would grow at a rate that would be less than the growth of the Gross Domestic Product. In other words, I would make sure that debt in relation to income did not increase.

But, in terms of specific programs, you know, I have no great ideas. I would probably - since I'm not running for office, and this is already scheduled to come in a couple of decades- I would probably extend the age at which Social Security kicks in, because I think the world is a lot different than in 1937 or whenever the retirement age was put in at 65. I think people are very productive at that age. If you look at demographics for people under 65 to support people over 65, it is a much different chore than it was 60 years ago. I just think there are more productive years, so I would have Social Security start somewhat later. That would save a lot of money. It would also not get the vote of the AARP or other organizations.

Q. I've heard that you feel that all universities should teach a course in common sense. I was just wondering: What is your definition of common sense? What should this course teach?
A. Well, I don't know whether I've said they ought to teach a course in common sense because I'm not sure you could teach it. But, I do find it amazing how many people with high IQs get off the track. It's astounding to me how people who are really very smart manage to engage in so many self-destructive actions, and I'm not just thinking in terms of business.
I have no real prescription, as I look around at the people whom I think are extremely sensible. I don't know quite how to transplant that or teach that to other people. I think a lot of people make things more complicated than they need to. There is nothing complicated about the way we invest. It is very understandable. I've felt that before people buy a stock, they should take a piece of paper and simply write, "I'm buying General Motors at 47," or "I'm buying US Steel at 83." They should just write out what their reasoning is, and they should be able to get it all on one side of one piece of paper. In fact, they should be able to get it into a paragraph. Almost all of the big, great ideas in business are very simple. Sam Walton's idea was very simple at Wal-Mart. It is not hard to do. If you want to accomplish something, and this ties in a little bit with common sense maybe, you have to have focus. Mrs. B had focus. Mrs. B never went to school a day in her life, and she ran rings around all kinds of people because she's smart and energetic. She was also focused. Tom Watson, who started IBM, was the same way. He said, "I'm no genius. I'm smart in spots, but I stay around those spots," and there is a lot to that.

Q. I'm a doctoral student in the School of Music, and my question has to do with arts funding. I'm wondering where you think the responsibility for funding for arts programs would lie. Would that be with governmental programs or with businesses or private individuals?

A. I think it's with government programs and private individuals. I mean, I think it's probably a combination needed on that. If you go back 50 or 75 years, it was entirely private. But I think, in terms of a lot of activities like that, there is a place for both the government and for private funding.

Q. I've heard that you refuse to assist your children financially. Is this true? And, what did you get from your parents financially?

A. Well, I got all kinds of good things. But, I didn't get money. And, I really didn't want it actually. I don't think I could have been raised with a better pair of parents. That was enormously important - I don't believe in making kids rich. I just think it's wrong in terms of society. I hear these people who lecture about the debilitating effects of food stamps on the poor.

They say, "You know, you give them food stamps, and they get dependent, and then the next generation wants more food stamps," and all that sort of thing. What is the difference between that and some kid who gets a lifetime supply of food stamps at birth through inheritance, you know, except the food stamps are called stocks and bonds and the welfare officer is called a trust officer? They never seem to see the debilitating effects of having some big trust fund for themselves.

I basically believe that if you are rich, you should leave your kids or give them enough so they can do anything but not enough so they can do nothing. I just think that makes sense. I don't think it should be like they were born into total poverty, and I don't think they should be entitled to live a life of doing nothing, essentially living off this stored-up supply of food stamps which somebody handed them. So, that is my own personal philosophy on it.

Q. Mr. Buffett, I would like to ask you about your political involvement. This year, we've seen a lot through the media of your being finance chair for Senator Kerrey and helping Congressman Hoagland in Omaha. My concern is, it seems like at least the business publications I read and the business organizations that I'm involved with aren't real supportive of those two individuals because of maybe increased taxes, regulation, and government-run health care. Can you explain to me your involvement with that and why you support those individuals that seem to be opposed to some business incentives?

(Aside, Mr. Buffett receives a can of Cherry Coke)

Sure. Thank you. This stuff will do wonders for you. If you are wondering, we get the profit from one out of every 14 of these, so it does my heart good.

A. I was president of the Young Republicans Club at the University of Pennsylvania in 1948 and, of course, grew up in a Republican household. I vote for plenty of Republicans, I mean, I'm not a card-carrying Democrat, although I'm a registered Democrat and have probably voted for more Democrats than Republicans. It would be pretty close. I don't like to get mixed up in politics much, but in this particular case, I've supported the two you mentioned for precisely the reason that some people are opposed to them. I felt that both Hoagland and Kerrey made a vote that they knew would be politically disadvantageous, perhaps even politically fatal. And, they did that for what they thought was for the benefit of society, whether you agree with them or not.

Now, that is the hardest thing in the world for a politician to do. It would be hard for me to do. I love the job of running Berkshire Hathaway. If I knew I was going to make some vote that might cause me to lose that job, I'm not sure how I would behave. So, I saw both of those fellows make a vote, and there was no question that it was going to hurt them politically. They had no problem assessing the mood of their own voters or voters around the

136

country. So, they did that and I thought that was exactly the way a legislator is supposed to behave. I felt it was very important I would have had a much different deficit reduction act than came forth, but that is not the question because you'll never be happy with every aspect of the bill. I felt it was important to the country that something be done at the time, and that was the bill to be voted on. It was a very close vote, as you know, and both of these fellows stood up and voted for it. So, I felt under those circumstances if I could help in any way by identifying with them, I would be delighted to do so. They stood up when it counted and I felt that I should, too. That's the reason, but basically I'm not big on getting involved in politics and it's not because they are Democrats. That's immaterial to me.

Q. You keep a very lean machine going at Berkshire Hathaway. How do you keep it so lean when it grows so much?

A. Well, that's a good question, because now we have 22,000 employees or maybe 23,000 or even 24,000, I guess. We probably had 1,000 twenty years ago but we've still got 10 or 11 people in headquarters. I really believe in keeping things simple. We have no inside counsel. We have no public relations people. We have no guards. We have no cafeteria. And, it's a lot easier to run that way. Frankly, I think way more gets done than if you have floor after floor of people that are reporting to people on the floor above them.

I see so much waste in most companies and once it gets there, it is very hard to get rid of. It's much easier never to get there. My pal Charlie says that, "All I want to know is where I'm going to die, so I'll never go there." And, that's the way I feel about a large organization. I mean, that would be business death as far as I'm concerned; so we're not going to get there. It's not a problem keeping it down. We just don't hire anybody and we won't.

I buy and sell all the stocks myself. Some people say, "How many people can you have reporting to you in a business?" That's standard organizational management stuff. They say, "The optimum number is this," or something like that. The answer is, if you've got the right kind of people, you can have tons of people. You can have dozens and dozens and dozens of people, if they know what they are doing and they like their jobs. But if you have somebody who's a clown, one is too many. They will drive you crazy. The trick is having the right people. We have been very fortunate in getting in with people who are extremely able at doing their jobs.

We bought H. H. Brown, which is a work shoe company, three years ago. It has probably 4,000 employees, and two hundred and fifty million dollars in sales. I've never been to one of their plants. No one ever has. Maybe they don't even exist. I mean, maybe those guys sit there every month and say, "What figures should we send Warren this month? $2.8 million, will he like that? Yeah, he'll probably like that; let's mail it to him." I've got the right kind of people. If you've got the Blumkins running the Furniture Mart or something, what can I do, you know? Should I go out there and tell them we should price this stuff at $498 retail instead of $398? I don't know anything about it.

Three-quarters of our managers are independently wealthy. They don't need to get up and go to work at all. Most of them have tens and tens of millions of dollars. So, I've got to create or I've got to maintain an environment where the thing they want to do most in the world is to go to work that day and the next day. And I say to myself, "What would make me feel that way?"

One way is to feel you are running your own show. If I had people second-guessing me all day, I would get sick of it. I would say, "What the hell do I need this for?" And, that's exactly the way our managers would feel if I went around second-guessing them or telling them how to run their business. So, you can get by with very few people if they are good people. That's what we try to do.

Q. You said that you look at three things when you are looking at a firm. You look at management, price and people. Is your analysis of people what makes your stock prices exceptional?

A. It's one of three, but it's all three things. I think I said the "economics" of the business. I mean, you can have the most wonderful person in the world, but if they are running a textile business like we had 30 years ago, they're not going to do well. On the other hand, if they're running Coca-Cola they are going to do sensationally. So, we want to be in a business that has fundamentally good economics like a Coca-Cola or a Gillette or something of the sort. And then we want people and the price. But all three are very important.

Q. I've come from a family where my father works a lot and he's rather successful. How do you balance work with your family? Do you tie your wife into any of your work, or is it totally two different dimensions, two different worlds?

A. No, it's two different deals. My daughter, who is here, was doing an interview one time and explained that when she was in high school, she told people I was a securities analyst. She thought that meant I went around checking on homes or something to be sure they wouldn't be burglarized!

No, work and family are two independent things. I don't consider what I do as work at all. I'm not doing this for a living. I'm doing it because I would rather do it than anything else I can think of in the world.

Q. You say in your annual report that you do not want to increase the number of investors you have through a stock swap or a split, but if you are in a sense a large mutual company, a large holding company, why would you not increase the amount of capital available to you?

A. Well, we haven't; we don't want to increase the amount of capital, which is different than increasing the number of shareholders, of course. We get a natural increase in capital just by the amount we earn from year to year, and that's plenty satisfactory. I do not have way more ideas than I have capital at the present. When I got out of school, I had way more ideas than capital. I was definitely capital short and at that point I did need more capital.

So that's why I formed a partnership in 1956 to have some partners join with me. But, Berkshire will not need new capital as we go along. Now, the question is, "Who are going to be your shareholders?" "Who is going to sit in every seat?" If you have a million shares outstanding, somebody has to own them, preferably me. All the seats get filled and then the question is,

"How do you encourage the people you want to have in those seats to attend?" It's very simple. If you stick a sign outside an auditorium and say "rock concert", you will get one group and if you say "opera", you will get another group. Either group is fine, but you'd better not have people coming who think they are going to the opera and find that they are at a rock concert, or vice versa.

So, I believe in communicating with the investment world about our objectives - how we think, and the time horizons to draw a compatible group into Berkshire - and we've done that over time. That's why the turnover in Berkshire stock is so low. We have less turnover than any stock on the New York Stock Exchange. The New York Stock Exchange doesn't like it but I like that because it means that basically the people are there who want to be there. Splitting the stock or anything like that would tend to draw a slightly different crowd; not a terrible crowd, but not a better crowd than the crowd we have already. The only way somebody can enter is for somebody to leave. And we want to make sure that we're not losing people who identified with our objectives and time horizons, to take on people who have some other different focus.

Q. What plans have you implemented for management succession when you and Mr. Munger slow down and retire?

A. Well, that's a polite way of saying when we die. We're not going to slow down and retire; we may slow down, but we won't retire. I'll put it that way because I plan to retire about five years after I die, actually. At the annual meeting somebody always says, "What happens if you...?", and then they stutter around a little bit and they finally get, "you know, you get hit by a truck?" I say, "Well, I'm glad you are asking that instead of asking what happens if you don't get hit by a truck." My job is fairly easy.

All of our operating businesses would continue just as they are. The people that are running H.H. Brown or Dexter or See's or Scott Fetzer, all know what they are doing. All I do is allocate capital. They mail me the money and then I use it to go buy something else. I also try to maintain conditions so that they want to keep working. I've got in mind people beyond the two of us who can fulfill that function.

I don't want to name them at present, but it's not as if Coca Cola (where we own almost $5 billion worth of it, close to 8% of the company) will change when I die. People are going to keep drinking Coke the day after; in fact they will probably toast me at the funeral with Coke and so sales may spurt a little bit! There's no big slowdown that will take place. The job of the person who succeeds me will be to take that money which keeps coming in and find intelligent things to do with it in the future.

Q. What kind of management training or mentoring do you believe in and actually practice at Berkshire?

A. Well, that's interesting. We really don't do any. Perhaps half of our managers have MBAs or have had other kinds of business training. Probably half of them didn't. It's interesting to me what makes a good manager, because I think you have to understand the language of business, and you should have what I would call a "business mind" or "business orientation." But, we don't care about background at all.

When I was at Salomon, I did not ask to see anyone's resume. I didn't know where any of the dozen went to school. It just didn't make a difference to me. You know, Mrs. B, if I asked her for her educational experience and she handed me a blank piece of paper, that would be fine with me. Ike Freidman, who built Borsheim's - I don't even know what he did in terms of school, or what he had done. It really is irrelevant to me.

We basically like to buy into businesses where people have already succeeded and then keep them on. I would much rather have somebody who has been batting .350 or .375, buy their business and try and keep them happy than have to go out and start casting around the sandlots looking for people who tell me they are going to bat .350 or .375. I'm not saying I won't do the latter. We've done some of the latter, but when you can do the former, we like it. We find it's hard to teach a new dog old tricks. We've got some terrific managers, many of whom are over 65 and many of whom did not have a business education.

I don't think a business education hurts, incidentally. I got one at Penn, Nebraska and Columbia, so I went to three different business schools and learned a lot at each place. Actually, I learned more at the last two. It can be quite advantageous, but I don't think it is essential.

Q. What do you feel is the best way to get money to pay for college?

A. The best way is to have somebody give it to you. Actually, my parents paid for my college education, so I did not. I worked for Mark Seacrest at the Lincoln Journal, but I took all that money and saved it to buy securities. You do it any way you can. If you've got a parent to give it to you, terrific. If you've got somebody that will give a scholarship to you, terrific. And, if you have to work for it, you know, that's what you have to do.

Q. I've heard the existence of a Buffett premium in regards to Berkshire Hathaway. Could you explain what that is and maybe comment on the reason for its existence?

A. Some people think we will do as well in the future as we have in the past. And, you can compare that to going out to the racetrack and betting on a 13-year-old horse that had a great record up to then. It's an extrapolation of the past and I don't think there is that much of a premium in it anyway, but that's just my own opinion.

Q. Mr. Buffett, I live in Los Angeles, California, which is generally regarded as being a horrible place to live anymore, but visiting my grandmother in Omaha, I find that the crime rate per capita is, I believe, worse than in Los Angeles. I don't know in the '50s and the '60s if crime was not such a forefront thing, but I'm wondering if you either politically or with your own personal fortune have any ideas on how to get us focused back on economic issues and not getting murdered on the way to the supermarket.

A. I don't necessarily want to accept the premise, and I'm not denying the premise. I just think when you compare the crime statistics of one community verses another, that can become quite tricky, because to some extent they are measuring the city, for example. Specifically, you become involved in how much of the population of the SMSA (Standard Metropolitan Statistical Area) is metropolitan in that city.

I have no great answer or fast answers to any crime problems. I think the most important single thing society can do something about - although it gets very tough if you've lost it - is to maintain an outstanding public school system. I think it's essential that everyone come as close to starting at the same starting point as possible in society.

Now, it isn't going to happen, because my kids are going to have all kinds of advantages that some low-income person's kids aren't going to have. And, there is a huge disparity. There is also a disparity in the talents they are born with. There is a disparity in the environment they have. But, there shouldn't be a disparity in the education they receive from society.

I think to the extent that one city after another - particularly the large ones - have lost a good public school system, that is a big contributing factor to a lot of social problems that follow. If I could do one thing, if I had a magic wand, I would try to figure out a way to have an outstanding public school system where there was no reason for anybody to send their kids, except for religious reasons, to private schools.

Private schools wouldn't be needed in order to get a good education. But I know Los Angeles's public school system, at least in many parts, has deteriorated. I have friends out there and they will pay lip service to a good public school system, but they will send their kids to private school, just like our legislators do in Washington, D.C. Essentially, I don't think there is anybody in Congress who sends their kids to the public schools. I went to public school in Washington, D. C. 40 years ago, and it was first class. We had half a dozen or more kids of Senators or Congressmen at that school. Today in Washington, public school students are not getting the same shot at the opportunities in America, if they have been forced into a system that is second-class. I don't have great solutions to this problem.

I know something about running business and investing, because I've been doing it for a long time. But, that does not give me great insight into a lot of the social problems of the day. One of the problems with philanthropy - and my foundation's board will have this problem with my funds - is that in business I get to solve the easy problems. I get to wait for fat pitches. I don't have to make a choice among 1,000 different companies. All I have to do is decide people are going to keep drinking Coke.

And, there is a lot of money to be made in manufacturing and distributing it. In philanthropy and in social situations, it's just the reverse. All of the intractable problems - the ones that are really tough to solve, the ones that take decades - are the ones that get thrown at you. That's why I do feel empathy for people in politics, because they are dealing with the toughest problems. They are dealing with problems that people couldn't solve last year, or the year before, or the year before that.

Regarding philanthropy, after I die, the Buffett Foundation will be tackling problems that are terribly important, but also terribly difficult to solve, and I wish them well. And I'll understand how important the requests are that they'll receive, and how terribly difficult it will be to solve, to make decisions, and I wish them well. But I'll understand; wherever I am I'll understand if they have difficulty accomplishing that.

Q. Mr. Buffett, how did you first get started and how did you deal with failure, if you had one?

A. How did I first get started? It depends. I bought my first stock when I was 11, but I'd been thinking about them for a long time before that. My dad was in the investment business and I used to go down to his office in the old Omaha National Bank building when I was seven or eight years old. I found out I was near-sighted because I couldn't read the quotations up on the stock board; otherwise I might have gone through life without glasses. I just got very interested in it. I started reading books on it when I was eight or nine and then I finally saved enough money to buy three shares of Cities Service preferred for $114 in 1942, and then I just kept doing it.

Failure depends on how you define it. A lot of things go wrong in life, but that doesn't necessarily mean that they're failures. I really don't look back. I try to learn from what I see around me, but I don't try to learn by going back over this decision or that decision or what did I do wrong or the sort. I don't think about that at all. You can make a lot of mistakes. The nice thing about it is you're going to make a lot of mistakes and still do very well. That's the encouraging thing. I write about my mistakes in the report. In fact, I have a section sometimes called "mistake du jour," and unfortunately it's plural most years, too.

It's not the end of the world. You don't want to make any ones that are fatal. You do not want to own securities on borrowed money because that can wipe you out. I've never borrowed money of any significant amount because I just didn't want to go back to go. Borrowed money can magnify your mistakes, and it may magnify them to the point where they wipe you out. But, there's nothing wrong with making mistakes. You should try to pick things that you understand.

That is the key to what I do. Occasionally I may make a mistake when I think I understand something I don't. Another mistake that you don't see is when I pass up something that I'm capable of understanding. Those are mistakes of omission and sometimes they have been huge. I could point to mistakes like that which have cost us over a billion dollars. I knew enough to do something but for one reason or another, I didn't. Fortunately, people don't see those.

Q. Mr. Buffet, after being the richest man in America, what are your major goals now?

A. Well, as I said at the Annual Meeting, now my goal is to be the oldest man in America. That's all I want said at my funeral. I just want someone to say, "My God, he was old!" I just want to keep doing what I'm doing, as long as I can. I have no desire to bring my golf handicap down five strokes particularly; it won't go down there by itself, and I'm not going to spend time to do it. It doesn't make that much difference to me. I feel like I can have as much fun doing what I do at this level as anything else. I really, really, really have no goals other than to stay healthy enough to keep doing the same thing I've been doing.

Q. I have a two-part question. Number one, what do you think about the future of the two-party system in America? And, number two, what do you think about the candidacy of Colin Powell for President in '96?

A. Well, what has happened, as you know, is that party identifications and loyalties have changed dramatically. I'm probably typical in that I may be registered one way or the other, but I don't really think much about that. Certainly there is no party discipline or loyalty that can be called upon to get me to vote for somebody whom I think is inferior to another candidate. I think television has contributed to that very substantially. I think the parties will continue along; I don't think they will disappear or splinter in all likelihood.

Everything I know about Colin Powell is good. I do not know him personally. He is clearly an outstanding human being. If he starts offering his opinions on various subjects, his popularity will tend to diminish because that's the nature of politics. When you have to say whether you are for or against something, you start losing people pretty fast. But, in terms of the quality of that individual, I would think he would be first-class. I have no idea really what his views are on a lot of subjects. We may learn in the next year or so.

Q. Mr. Buffett, you said that people who are better off than society have a debt to society. I find this respectable. I just am wondering, what's your debt?

A. Well, I really think in terms of material goods that overwhelmingly eventually belong to society. I think it would be obscene if I tried to consume them all myself or have my family consuming like crazy forever just because I happen to be well adjusted to this society. The interesting thing is that we live in a market society.

If you can bat .375, if you can shoot sub-par golf, if you can do what I do, if you have certain kinds of talents, the market will pay enormously for those talents. Now, it didn't pay that well for ballplayers 25 years ago because the stadiums only held 50,000 people, but television and cable have made it possible for the stadiums to hold 250 million people and that changes the economics dramatically.

This market system showers rewards on people with certain types of talents. Yet it does not shower rewards on other people with talents just as important to society, maybe more important to society. An outstanding teacher, outstanding nurse or researcher may not be paid dramatically more and maybe no more than the mediocre one. But the outstanding heavyweight fighter, or the outstanding center fielder, or the outstanding stock picker, or whoever, gets incredibly more because of the way the market system works.

I would not tamper with that market system, because I do think that people benefit, because it delivers the goods that people want in this country. It has been a great system for causing an outpouring of goods and services that people want. The market system works terrifically that way. I don't think it works terrifically in terms of distribution of the rewards. And, I think you solve that in two ways. One way is you solve it through your tax system and the other way is you solve it through philanthropy. You might call this a self-imposed tax. I think you could probably find 300 public school teachers in Omaha who have contributed absolutely as much to society as some fellow like myself, or somebody that bats .350, or some guy that has won the light-heavyweight boxing championship.

The teachers are never going to get paid properly. Society will not reward them that way. I don't see any way for society to do that. I don't have anything in mind about some "comparable worth" type of arrangement. I think the market system is the best system for delivering goods, but then I think in terms of distributing these goods and services produced by that market system. Both philanthropy and a progressive tax system of some sort are the appropriate methods.

Q. My question concerns something that has come to the forefront in the last couple of years in politics especially - environmental issues. We have seen an increase in the concern of this country, and around the world, with environmental issues. People say a lot of the environmental problems are a result of businesses taking technologies that are not so benign to the environment and applying them in negative ways. In your opinion, as a corporate industrial leader, what would be some criteria that should be established so that corporations could find ways to apply more benign technologies?

A. I would say on environment that we've already got legislation in place which makes it extremely painful for companies who are doing things which are environmentally harmful.

I don't know all the details, but I've seen enough of the Environmental Protection Agency's operation that I think that situation has changed dramatically from 25 years ago, at least in this country. What we do about the rest of the world is another question.

In a world economy, to the extent that you apply any kind of restrictions, in terms of child labor or environment or workers compensation that other countries don't impose, you have a competitive cost disadvantage. That's a price that society has to pay here, but it is a real cost.

I personally think that population is probably one of the most important issues the world faces, except for the eventual problem of nuclear proliferation. I don't know how much the proper population of the world should be or will be. I know that number is different from what it would have looked like hundred years ago, and it probably will look different a hundred years from now. But, I do know there is a number and it may be affected by technology and it may be affected by the fact that our resources are greater than we think now.

If we in this room were to all embark on a space ship journey some place, which was going to last a hundred years, and they were going to put provisions in the space ship that would be ample for this group, we might not know how many more people we could take on that space ship before we endangered the ability to survive and return in a hundred years. But we would know that the number was finite.

And, we would certainly err on the low side. We would not say, "Well, let's just take a shot at it and have 500 more join us." It is a finite world. Man's imagination is not necessarily finite, and we can do a lot of things that we haven't even thought of with resources. But in the end, there is only so much oil and gas in the ground. We're dealing with finite resources. They're not known, but they are finite. I would say it is a terrible mistake for the human race to test what the ultimate carrying capacity of this planet is. We had better have a margin of error. I believe that population is a terribly important issue.

Now, one of the problems in society is that the most important issues are often these incremental type things. The world is not going to come to an end because tomorrow there are 200 or 250 thousand more people on the planet than there were today. That's about the number it grows every day. There is nothing apocalyptic about it. People will go on making apocalyptic projections. But, it is like eating about 300 calories more each day than you burn up; it has no effect on you today.

You don't get up from the table and all of a sudden everybody says, "My God, you look fat compared to when you sat down!" But, if you keep doing it over time, the incremental problems are hard to attack because that one extra piece of pie doesn't really seem to make a difference. The 250,000 people tomorrow don't seem to make any difference, but the cumulative effects of them will make a huge difference over time, just like overeating will make a huge difference over time. The time to attack those problems is early. It's a huge determiner of the kind of environment we have. I think the time to be thinking about those issues is now.

Q. Mr. Buffett, two of the Berkshire holdings that you have were mentioned today, Coke and Gillette. Another company that has repeat daily sales like that is Wrigley. Why has Berkshire not purchased that and what would make you purchase Wrigley?

A. Well, I won't comment on whether we own or don't own anything. I mean, there are certain holdings we have to show in our report, but we don't have to show all of our holdings. There are certain threshold levels, but Wrigley is obviously a strong worldwide franchise. How you may feel about the growth in units sales in chewing gum verses the growth in units sales of soft drinks is one question.

How you may feel about the pricing flexibility that they have verses the pricing flexibility that Coke or Gillette may have is another. And then how you feel about the price of a stock in the company would be a major factor. I'm not going to get specific on Wrigley because I don't get specific on stocks. But, it clearly has the kind of worldwide recognition that we like.

In the case of Gillette, they improve the product periodically. I hope you buy a new Sensor Excel because it produces a very smooth shave! The ticker abbreviation used to be "GS" on the New York Stock Exchange, which stood for "good shave". There are about 21 billion blades sold every year. Gillette sells only about 7 billion of them, but they've got about 60% value share because they've done it technologically. The Sensor took 11 years to develop; that is really some product. One thing you'd find interesting: the Sensor for women has become a very big product. More Sensor for women razors were sold in the first 18 months than Sensors were sold originally in their first 18 months.

That's the first time a razor's become remotely that popular with women. Normally, women use disposables or they use their husband's or boyfriend's razor. But, one thing research has shown, which is kind of interesting (those of you in the audience will take this several ways): When a man gets a nick or a scrape or cuts himself with a razor, he blames the razor. But when a women does, she blames herself and that enters into the kind of product she wants to buy.

It is also true, of course, there's only about one-tenth of the nerve receptors per square centimeter in the leg than there are in the face. So, the man tends to be more sensitive to the feel of the shave, and the women is more sensitive to whether she gets nicks or scrapes on her legs. (There are all kinds of interesting things about razors.) People originally started shaving with rocks because it was a disadvantage in combat with other humans or animals to have something the enemy could grab you by and snap your neck with. That's diminished over the years, but that was the original reason.

Q. Mr. Buffett, in recent years several public accounting firms have been sued by their clients because they have not met their expectations on their auditing services. I was wondering what you and Berkshire Hathaway expect from your external auditors?

A. Well, that's a good question. I said to the Federal Financial Accounting Standards Boards some years ago that I thought accountants deserved to be sued, because I thought the typical accountant certificate in those days was overstated. I did not think they were in a position in many companies to deliver that opinion and when they have been held financially accountable for the fact that they couldn't back up that opinion, I really thought that was appropriate. It may have gone overboard in some cases, but they were stating something there that people relied on. In many cases - take banks or insurance companies - they were simply not in a position to attest as they did.

In our own case, we are small and controlled, and we have an internal audit staff. I'm hoping, if an outside auditor comes up with anything, it may be a potential tax idea, or it might be things our internal auditors did not spot in terms of weaknesses in the control system, or they might spot outright fraud of some sort. We haven't had that, but that's what I'm paying them to do, aside from the fact I have to have them anyway because I'm required to by the Securities and Exchange Commission and the New York Stock Exchange. Incidentally, we have bought big firms that never had an audit, and that doesn't bother me.

When I made the deal with Mrs. Blumkin, it was on August 30, 1983. I know that because it was my birthday. I didn't want to tell her that early on, because I thought she might think I was over-eager. I told her afterwards and she said, "You bought an oil well on your birthday!" She had no audit and she just told me she owned all the land, all the buildings. and all the inventory. She told me about what the receivables were, what the business was about, that all the bills were paid, and they didn't owe any money. We never had an audit. We bought that business with a contract that was one page long.

Q. Do you have any opinions or predictions on how health care reform is going to affect the economy, in general, and Berkshire Hathaway, specifically?

A. Well, as I said earlier, we had our one general meeting on health care about six or seven years ago. When you are spending 14% of the Gross Domestic Product on something that other countries are spending 9% or less, it affects your competitive position. You would like to feel that you are getting a whole lot more for your money. I have no idea how the debate is going to come out because you are talking about one-seventh of the economy and something that is emotionally charged, I do think the rate of increase in health cost has dampened considerably, but I don't think that is necessarily permanent. I think it can last for a few years and it will come back if we start getting increases in health care costs significantly above the general rate of inflation. You are going to hear a lot about health care, again, and you should.

Q. You say that you don't like to look at resumes. What do you think businesses that do use them find impressive about resumes?

A. Well, I would say that, if you are talking about the typical large business, they look at labels. In other words, it you get an MBA, you have the label MBA. If you get it from a certain place, you know, it says that, too. There is an awful lot of hiring done based on that. The label definitely has an economic value. I can't quantify that exactly, but it has a significant economic value. It just doesn't happen to have it with us. But if you are getting hired by IBM or General Motors or Merrill Lynch, it's going to make a difference in the way they look at you initially. I don't think it makes that much difference five years out. But I do think it makes a difference in starting salary. It makes a difference in your likelihood of getting hired for a great many positions. Then, it's really what you show from that point forward. But it is a very useful label in getting hired by a large company.

We don't even think of ourselves as a large company. We think of ourselves as a collection of medium-sized companies. Incidentally, we've got a fellow that runs one of our larger subsidiaries; an MBA might mean quite a bit to him. And he's the one that hires for the group. I do no hiring, except if the top person in one of our companies dies or retires. I make maybe one hiring decision every three years. They also make hiring decisions all the time, and I don't get into what criteria they use. That's entirely up to them. I don't see how you can hold somebody responsible for an operation and then start telling them how to hire people. We have no human resources department at Berkshire.

Some of our subsidiaries have somebody in that position, but we have nobody at the top who in turn supervises all that. Most companies do and once they do, they start building empires. They start going to all the conventions and seminars, and then they hire assistants to do this, and it just goes on and on. So we don't start it. Two more questions, okay?

Q. Mr. Buffett, this question deals with international investment. Since you are a key person in your corporations, when you make decisions on important international portfolios, what kind of factors come into your mind when selecting a nation to invest in? What do you think about China as a "hot market" right now?

A. Well, we like companies, obviously, that have big international potential. But we're perfectly willing to buy into a company that can never go outside the region. Nebraska Furniture Mart is not going to sell anything internationally, although they will sell a lot throughout the Midwest. It's just one variable that enters in. Gillette just bought 70% of the Shanghai Razor Company, which is the largest razor company over there. Coke will sell 135 million cases this year in China, which is only two per capita, roughly, as compared to 325 per capita in the United States.

That's very encouraging and they are moving very fast in China. One problem Gillette has is that the Chinese do not shave as often as Americans. But we plan to put something in Coke to change that!

Q. You support a progressive consumption tax policy. I think your idea is the best and works when our economy is booming or overheated. What do you think if our economy is in a severe recession like in 1981-82?

A. A progressive consumption tax, if enacted, would hurt the economy in the following year or maybe a couple of years, regardless of when it was introduced, simply because if we are consuming 100% of the goods produced in the country and all of the sudden you say we're going to start saving 5%, that would take consumption down to 95%, assuming no immediate increase in output, which there wouldn't be. If you're making $5,000 a month and you decide to save more in your family, you're going to cut consumption at that point. Later on, you may increase consumption because of the product of that investment.

Any kind of a consumption tax that induces more investment will hurt the economy in the following year or two, which makes it tough to sell. That makes it tough to sell in your own household, too. If you say we're going to start saving more and consuming less, that's not necessarily a winning argument. But it is the way to build wealth over time. I would say no matter when it was introduced, it would have a bite for a while.

Think back to 1790, when 90% of the people in the country were on farms. If some guy had come along and said we're going to develop tractors, combines, and cultivators that will put 80% of these people out of work so that a small percentage of people will be on farms, people would say, "That's terrifying, you know, we can't have that." Actually, saving and investment frees up people to do all kinds of other things, as you have seen on the long scale of 200 years of this country.

It's a terrifying prospect to people in the short run, because they see the unemployment; they don't see those people being freed up to produce all kinds of other things over time. If you could have had a little video tape that you showed all the farmers in the country in 1790, and said, "Use this one tractor instead of needing all of your sons and sons-in-law and everybody else to farm this place, and you will be able to do it yourself. The other eight people will be unemployed," I would have hated to have a referendum on whether people wanted progress, in terms of better farm machinery. That is the problem with increasing the investment rate in the country. And, in a politically charged environment with sound bites on television, I'm not sure it could be sold.

Well, I want to thank you all for coming; it's been a real pleasure to return to the University of Nebraska and I hope we keep our quarterbacks healthy. Thanks.

Recommended Readings

- The Anatomy of Success, Nicolas Darvas

- The Dale Carnegie Course on Effective Speaking, Personality Development, and the Art of How to Win Friends & Influence People, Dale Carnegie

- The Law of Success In Sixteen Lessons (Complete, Unabridged), Napoleon Hill

- It Works, R. H. Jarrett

- The Art of Public Speaking (Audio CD), Dale Carnegie

- The Success System That Never Fails (Audio CD), W. Clement Stone

- How I Made $2,000,000 In The Stock Market, Nicolas Darvas

- The Battle for Investment Survival, Gerald M. Loeb

- You Can Still Make It In The Market, Nicolas Darvas

- Technical Analysis of Stock Trends, Robert D. Edwards

Available at www.bnpublishing.net